D1431178

Awarded
The Catholic Writers Guild Seal of Approval
2011

Come My Beloved:

Inspiring Stories of Catholic Courtship

Edited by Ellen Gable Hrkach
and Kathy Cassanto

Ellen Gable Hrkach

Full Quiver Publishing, Pakenham, Ontario

Come My Beloved:
Inspiring Stories of Catholic Courtship
copyright by Full Quiver Publishing
PO Box 244
Pakenham, Ontario
K0A 2X0

ISBN Number: 978-0-9736736-1-6
Printed and bound in Canada
Cover design and photography by
James Hrkach

Scripture texts are taken from the Douay Version of the Holy Bible

NATIONAL LIBRARY OF CANADA CATALOGUING IN
PUBLICATION

Gable Hrkach, Ellen 1959 -
Cassanto, Kathy 1970 -
Come My Beloved: Inspiring Stories of Catholic Courtship
ALL RIGHTS RESERVED

"Come my beloved, let us go forth into the field,
let us abide in the villages."
Canticle of Canticles 7:11

"... if you love until it hurts, there can be no more hurt, only
love."
Blessed Mother Teresa

"Love...love...love...never counting the cost."
"The Little Mandate"
Catherine Doherty, Foundress of Madonna House

Since the beginning of human history, romantic love has been a frequent topic of songs, books, poems, plays and movies. One need only look at the popularity of romance novels and love songs to realize that our fascination with romantic love and the ideal "love story" is, in some sense, an expression of the desire to see that it all ends "happily ever after."

In the secular world, romantic love has taken the form of a mere feeling. "If it feels good, do it" or "I just don't love you anymore" are just some of the prevalent philosophies today. With these attitudes, separation and divorce have become the norm.

Posie Douthwright has a beautifully accurate description of falling in love, the kind that sees love as more than just a feeling. In the story of the courtship with her husband, David, she says, "I think of falling in love as more like falling into God together, and allowing His love to be made manifest between us." (p. 26)

"I promise to be true to you in good times and in bad, in sickness and in health. I will love you and honor you all the days of my life." When husband and wife recite, and physically express, those vows, God's love truly becomes manifest.

For couples who have journeyed through 'good times' and 'bad times' together, love becomes much more than being "in love." True love or "falling into God together" develops into a conscious decision to selflessly live the marriage vows to the fullest no matter what the circumstances. This type of love is one that grows in strength and is rarely vulnerable to the degradation of the modern threats of 'falling out of love.'

The idea for this book came about on Valentine's Day two years ago. A group of mothers were enjoying one another's fellowship as our children played and exchanged cards. We began sharing how each of us met our husbands. One by one we recounted our stories. It became evident that God's hand *was* truly and firmly present in bringing each couple together. Kathy Cassanto, one of the mothers present, remarked, "It's too bad there isn't a book available with Catholic courtship stories." My initial response was, "Well, if there isn't, there should be."

Later that day, I went online and discovered that there appeared to be no books containing Catholic courtship/dating stories. So I asked Kathy to be my co-editor, and we set out to find inspiring Catholic courtship stories. Oftentimes, I simply listened to a small quiet voice prompting me to ask a particular couple, "Would you be willing to share how the two of you met?"

We agreed that the easiest and fastest way to gather the stories was to interview the couples, transcribe the interviews and edit them. Most of the stories in this book were from recorded conversations, then transcribed and edited, although a few were written by the couples themselves.

As I interviewed each couple, a clear picture began to emerge: that true love was far different – and in many cases, more interesting – than the infatuation which is so often portrayed in movies and books.

Each of these courtship/dating stories has its own theme, but all of them illustrate that God is the ideal matchmaker. The stories are uplifting, inspirational, humorous, hopeful, romantic.

Mother Teresa's quote "...*if you love until it hurts, there can be no more hurt, only love,*" can help prepare couples that the notion of an earthly "happily ever after" is possible, but not without the sacrificial self-giving decision to love.

Ellen Gable Hrkach, editor
June 15, 2011

Table of Contents

Michel and Jeanette MacDonald

Married September 19, 1998

Your Vocation is Hidden in Your Baptism

Jeanette and Michel 1998

Jeanette: I think that God is a God of waiting. But when He chooses to act, it's like lightning. When I was 31, in October '97, I had just moved back in with my parents in New Jersey and I had recently gotten a job teaching. But for ten years previous to this, I had been waiting for a husband. I really thought I'd be married at age 21, which I was not. I felt positive that I was called to marriage and I had dated a few guys, but up until this point, nothing had worked out. I was still waiting for my husband. And I really could not understand why God would make me wait that long. So I started to think, *Well, maybe I've just missed the boat. Maybe I have a different vocation.*

So I talked to a priest, Father Peter, for a little direction and he invited me to a talk he was giving on baptism. He told me that I would find my vocation in my baptism; that each person's call is rooted in his or her baptism.

To assure myself that I wasn't just running away from religious life, I decided to write to a convent of nuns that I admired. I received their questionnaire and started to fill it out. When I got to the question, "What do you most want to do with your life?" I thought, *Get married and have lots of kids.* I never sent in the form.

I prayed, "God, what do you want me to do while I'm sitting here waiting and waiting for my husband?"

As I prayed, I felt the answer was to focus on my music (I had written some songs). Throughout the fall term, I began working on some new songs I had written, adding introductions, fixing the lyrics, et cetera. I decided with my brother, Terry, who was a seminarian up in Canada, to record some of these songs on something better than a little tape player.

Michel: Just by way of introduction, I had been away from the Church for several years and had a dramatic return the Christmas of 1991. I then spent a year in prayer and formation, eight months of which were at Madonna House in Combermere, Ontario in their spiritual formation program for men discerning the priesthood. After that, I joined the Companions of the Cross in Ottawa.

Of the five years that I was with the Companions, the first two years were a really graced moment in my life where I felt that God was calling me to the priesthood. My third year, I hit a brick wall. I did not want this call to the priesthood and it was something that I fought with my whole being. After struggling for a year, I was able to surrender to God and say, "Okay, well, if this is what you're calling me to, then I'll continue on this journey. But if it's not what you're calling me to, then you'll obviously close the door and open another door." I was very much at peace with where God wanted me to be.

In the Fall of '97, it was the beginning of my fifth year as a seminarian when Jeanette came up to Ottawa the week of American Thanksgiving. Our friend Randa held a Thanksgiving dinner and invited some of the Companions seminarians. This is where I met Jeanette.

Jeanette: After dinner, I took out my guitar and Terry and Michel joined me in playing some music. We played quite a few of my songs. It was fun. I thought, *This is nice to be sharing some of my music with these people,* because music had become a central theme in my life.

Michel: I found Jeanette's songs very profound. During the song called "As I Run," she sang, "Which hand will I hold as I run toward you, running to the light of Your Glory... Is this hand the one to grasp tighter as we lift each other to You?"

As she sang this song, something happened deep within my heart. I thought, *I want to be the one to run with her and to lift her up.* It was a profound movement in my soul and in my heart. It wasn't like *Oh, I'm in love with this girl this week.* I didn't even really know Jeanette. Yet somehow I had this really strong movement within me.

So in my prayer time, I was journaling, saying, is this what's going on? Is my heart fickle? Am I being distracted here? Here is this person who is very deep, spiritual, has a great love for You and is musical, funny and who, for all intents and purposes, would make a perfect wife. Yet I was on this journey towards the priesthood.

As part of the Companions' formation, you take part in small share groups with your brother seminarians. I told these men in my share group how I felt, that this was something very profound. I also confided my feelings to my spiritual director. He said that this needed to be seriously discerned. He made it very specific: Should I marry Jeanette? That was the question. So it was...am I called to the priesthood or should I marry Jeanette? When you get married, you're getting married to one person and so my spiritual director made it very specific.

I then began using the Ignatian discernment method.

This usually takes the form of a 30-day retreat where you meditate on various Gospel readings. I didn't do a 30-day retreat. I did a shortened version called Annotation 19 which takes place over a longer period of time – several months. With my spiritual director, I used the Ignatian method to discern whether I should get married to Jeanette. At the same time, I was very open with the men in my share group. Also, as this was going on, because it was something very deep and very profound and it also had serious consequences, I had people praying for me. If I met people whom I trusted and knew well, I told them to pray for me because I was discerning whether this truly was my vocation, this call to the priesthood with the Companions of the Cross.

Jeanette: Now we're into January, 1998. At this point, my brother and I decided to invite a few friends to help with this little recording project we were going to do. So we invited Michel to play on the guitar and another seminarian, Dan, on drums. We asked a friend, Marie, to sing, Lucy to play the piano, and our friends Randa and John to help out with some other things. We were preparing for the recording project and I made a demo of all the songs so that everybody could learn them. The recording week was in February of 1998. It turned out that this was my spring break from teaching and it was also Terry and Michel's spring break from their studies.

During this week I traveled up to Ottawa. Terry, Michel and I practiced every day for the upcoming recording session which was going to happen on the weekend. I knew Michel a bit from talking to him when I had gone up to see my brother. Throughout this week, I started to really, really like him. He was very good looking, a man of God and a man of prayer. One time I went into an adoration chapel to pray for an hour and he was there when I came in and he was still there when I left. I remember that specifically. And he was also a great guitar player. Being a musician, it's this that really attracted me to him. Michel basically had all these qualities that I was looking for in a husband. But there was only one problem: he was unavailable. He was a seminarian. I thought, *Great, another dead end street. Everything's becoming a dead end street.*

During this week, Michel had mentioned to us as a group to pray for him, because he was discerning whether or not to stay with the Companions of the Cross. I figured he might just as easily join some other group of priests. I did, however, write in my journal that I wanted to marry a man like Michel MacDonald.

It turned out the recording weekend was a big high. It was so much fun and we were all totally exhausted, but it was just a wonderful week and a wonderful weekend with everybody. I was staying at Randa's house with Lucy and Marie and we called a few of the guys to see if they would join us for breakfast. We called Michel and I was so happy that he came over. He had breakfast with us, right before I left to go back home to New Jersey. So even though I really liked him, he was unavailable, but it was just nice to know that this type of man actually did exist.

Michel: In the Ignatian method of discernment, what you're seeking out is God's will for your life, that which will bring Him greater glory. You really have to try as best as humanly possible to be indifferent in discerning to which state of life you are called. Obviously, I was in the seminary and I had feelings for Jeanette, but I had to be reserved. I didn't want to make known my feelings for her because I was discerning something and the whole point of being indifferent is trying to come to the space of being open to God's will.

The recording week was great. Afterwards, it was kind of a let down because it had been a very intense week. I was very sad that Jeanette left. My feelings for her were really strong and deep.

You have to know Jeanette. After the recording, she had sent this band newsletter to all the people who had been part of the project. Jeanette is very bubbly and outgoing.

I forget what was in the band newsletter, but it was very bubbly. Also she wrote to me once.

Jeanette: I sent everybody in the band a thank you card.

Michel: She sent a thank you card and in the card she asked for a copy of a song that I had written, and she asked about my sister. When I wrote back to her, I sent her the tape and I said, basically, you're welcome, here's my tape and my sister is doing well, thanks, bye. Before I sent it, I shared it with the men in my share group. I didn't want to lead her on or let her know my feelings for her, because I was in the process of discernment. So I just answered the questions in a polite, but terse, short letter.

Jeanette: After I had requested this song and before he sent it, I had to go back up to Canada. I think we forgot to record some vocals or we were picking the cover or something like that. So I saw Michel and he hadn't answered my letter yet, so I teased him about it. "You never sent me the song." He just seemed very serious and he said, "I did send it to you." "You did? Really? I haven't gotten it yet." He said, "I sent it to you."

He seemed really serious and a little annoyed or uncomfortable or something. It was just strange. I was surprised that he actually sent it, because guys don't generally write letters. When I returned home and got it, I had kind of mixed feelings because he had written a really short note.

Now, let's skip ahead to Easter time. I was blessed with the opportunity to go to France with Randa for Easter. We traveled around and we got to visit Jeunesse Lumière, a school of prayer and evangelization in France. Randa and my brother, Terry, had started a school like this in Canada called Youth Blaze. I had been a leader on Youth Blaze and Michel had been a leader the summer before.

During the Easter visit, we also got to go to Lisieux. I love St. Thérèse of Lisieux. At Lisieux, I prayed hard. I basically said, "Lord, this is your last chance. If I really have missed out on what I'm supposed to do, if I really have a vocation to the Carmelites, then you have got to let me know here. This would be the most appropriate place."

So I prayed that God would show me and I received absolutely nothing, no word, no confirmation that I should become a Carmelite, no leading towards that whatsoever. So I thought, *Okay. I guess it is still marriage, so where is my husband?*

Michel: I had been doing the Ignatian discernment, and at some point, you make what is called the election. You make your choice. Then you have another week of prayer and discernment to confirm the election. So I went down to Rhode Island to a friend of the Companions of the Cross, Father Jake Randall, a friend of Father Bob Bedard (the founder of the Companions of the Cross). I went with another seminarian to take the time of Holy Week to pray for the confirmation of my election. It was confirmed in my prayer throughout my discernment that yes, I should marry Jeanette.

The thing with Ignatian discernment is that you must have complete abandonment and trust in the Lord regarding the outcome. I had to be prepared that even if I had discerned properly, it didn't necessarily mean that it was God's will for me to marry Jeanette. She could say to me, "Listen, you're off your rocker." Then what? I would have to leave the Companions because I had discerned the call to marriage. I'd be kind of left holding the bag. But that is something that the Lord could allow for my growing closer to Him. I had to realize that if everything fell apart, I would have to completely abandon myself to Him, and trust that He was leading me somewhere unknown. So that was also what was going on in my mind.

Anyway, I discerned and I prayed and my spiritual director confirmed my decision.

At Easter week, I came back to Ottawa after having spent Holy Week and Easter in Rhode Island.

Jeanette: Here we come to the second Sunday of Easter, Divine Mercy Sunday, April 19th, 1998. I will never forget this day as long as I live.

In the morning, I remember I was praying and I was really saying, "Lord, come on. Fulfill my vocation. This is ridiculous. This has been a long enough wait, please." I wrote in my journal. "If you don't come soon, my box of tears will fill over. Fulfill my vocation. It is marriage. I'm positive of that. Send me my husband. Please, Lord, marriage is my vocation. It was confirmed in Lisieux. When will you fulfill it? Fulfill my vocation."

Out of all that prayer, I ended up writing a song that morning called "Fulfill My Vocation."

That's what happened in the morning. Later on in the day, I decided to call everyone in the band because I wanted to invite them over to my parents' house, which is on a lake. Most of the people were not home so I left messages. Then I called my brother, and he told me that that weekend would not work out well for him. So I had to call everyone back.

Michel: Jeanette had phoned and had left a message. I phoned back, but I think the phone was busy. So I thought, *Well, I won't do anything. I'll just pray a rosary and wait for her to contact me.* She ended up phoning. I was praying at the time, and that's when I let her know I couldn't go to her parents' place because it was during exam time and all that. Then we spoke about our Easter experiences.

Jeanette: I was glad Michel was actually at home. We chatted for an hour or so, how was your Easter, how was your trip to Rhode Island, how was your trip to France? We just kept talking. I thought to myself, *Well, I don't have to go. I'm not going to hang up. If he wants to talk to me, great.* So after an hour of talking about different things, he said, "Well, I've made a decision about the Companions."

I said, "Wow, that's great. How do you feel about that?

That must be a big decision that you've made."

He was quiet, but then he said to me, "You have something to do with it." At this point, you have to understand, I have no idea that he likes me other than as a friend. So when he said that, I thought to myself, *Oh, gee, I must have said something profound. Maybe I gave him a word of wisdom that God used in his discernment, or something like that.* That's actually what I was thinking at that moment.

Then he said to me, "I feel called to marriage and not just marriage to anyone, but marriage to you." At this point, I was in complete shock, complete, complete shock. But I was absolutely thrilled! "Great, that's wonderful!" I don't remember exactly what I said, but I was just so happy. I could not believe it.

It reminds me of this quote from The Jeweler's Shop, which is a play written by Karol Wojtyla, Blessed John Paul II. In it, he said, "Love can be a collision." That is exactly what it felt like. It was a collision. It was like crash, bam. God drops my husband down from heaven, right in front of me. Here you go. Here's your husband you've been waiting for for ten years.

Michel: I did share with her that I was leaving the Companions and that she had something to do with it and I felt called to marriage with her. She was ecstatic and so was I.

Jeanette: After, we hung up. We were actually talking on the phone through the 3:00 Divine Mercy hour. I still have the phone bill. After we hung up, my dad came home from wherever he was, and I remember saying to him, "Dad, this is the best day of my life." Then I told him that I was going to get married. I think he was a little surprised, but he was very happy for me.

I didn't tell anyone except my parents, because I was still trying to absorb all of this. After about a week, I shared it with some people that I worked with and they were absolutely in shock. They said, "You've got to be kidding. Last week, you weren't even dating anyone and now you're going to get married?"

But I really had no doubt. I was so sure, even though I didn't know Michel very well, to tell you the truth. We spent a week together on the recording project but other than that, we hardly spent any time in the same room. However, I was sure that this was the right thing. Also, I knew that my brother and Randa knew him well. Both of them and other people that I knew thought very highly of Michel.

Michel: Her brother had said at one point to John, another seminarian who is now a priest with the Companions, that the type of person suitable for Jeanette would be someone who was like a Companions of the Cross seminarian, someone with that same spirituality.

Basically, our courtship was that we spoke on the phone practically every single night. We also wrote letters. When Jeanette came up two weeks later, she brought her great-grandmother's wedding ring and I proposed to her.

Then I went down to see Jeanette in New Jersey. On the way, I stopped at my sister's house in Massachusetts. She gave me my mother's engagement ring. When I saw Jeanette, I gave her the engagement ring, and then we went to visit her grandfather in the hospital. He said, "Oh, so this is the real deal. You got the ring and the whole bit."

We were married five months later on September 19, 1998 and we now have seven beautiful kids.

Jeanette: If you recall from the beginning of our story, I talked about Father Peter, whom I had gone to see. He had said, "You will find your vocation in your baptism." I was baptized on Easter Sunday in 1966, which is April 10th. Well, lo and behold, Michel's birthday is April 10th, 1966, so he was born on the very day that I was baptized. It was so amazing. Father Peter's words ended up being prophetic in that sense, this real connection between Michel and I.

Michel teaches theology and Jeanette is a full-time mother to their seven children, ages one year to 11 years old. They live near Ottawa, Ontario.

The MacDonald Family

David and Posie Douthwright

Married December 31, 2004

You Should Get Married Again

David and Posie 2004

Posie: I had been widowed for seven years when David came along, and I still had two children at home. My first husband had a real sense of humor and, although he didn't know he was going to die until fairly close to his death, he had a feeling, and he used to tell me, "You know, if I die, you should get married again." It was sort of a joke, but serious too, sincerely reassuring me that's what he would want for me.

Anyway, God wanted me to be a single parent for seven years. I'm sure He knew what was best, but I was starting to wonder whether God did have someone for me. I still felt called to the married state, and I loved being married, but I wasn't going to go out looking.

My faith was tested and strengthened by losing my first husband, and I don't know how I would have done it without my faith. That call to marriage was really strong in me, and yet God reveals Himself in His own time and in His own way.

I accepted the fact that God wanted me to be celibate if I wasn't married, but was He calling me to a life of prayer? As my children were growing up, what was I going to do?

I had known David for 20 years before this because he had come to our retreat center with his family, David and Anna and their six children.

David: I had lost my wife almost two years before Posie came along. I had no children living at home at the time. One thing that became really paramount for me, more than at any other time in my marriage with Anna, was that I needed to get my faith in order. So the discipline that really kind of saved my life during that time after Anna died was really strengthened, and God gave me the grace to try and be more disciplined in prayer and reading. Church has always been important, but just my private time for strengthening my faith became a lot stronger. And I thank God for that because I was fairly well-grounded when I met Posie again. I was living at our family cottage at the time, just outside Barry's Bay, Ontario. Posie was living in Combermere. I used to come to the local parish where Posie attended Mass, and our friendship was present already, so it was nice to start with that friendship basis and the commonality of the Nazareth Retreat Center that she and Don had directed. It was a tremendous common experience to have had that time spent with our families at the Nazareth Family Retreat Centre.

Posie: When I thought about getting married again, I had no idea how that could happen; I just couldn't really imagine. Certainly I couldn't go down the road that so many single people go down, going to bars and trying to find a man. I knew it would have to be God sending someone to me. When He didn't, after that number of years, I started to wonder about it. "Well, what *is* my call? My kids will be leaving soon, and I'm going to be rattling around in this house here."

As part of my discernment, it just worked out that someone anonymously gave me this amazing gift of a trip to Medjugorje in 2004. I was so thrilled and felt so confirmed and cared for, that someone would do this for me. On that trip, part of my discernment was "God, show me; Our Lady, show me. If you have anyone for me, tell me. And if you don't, tell me that, too. And I'll follow wherever you want me to go, whatever life that you ask of me."

During that pilgrimage, I really felt God saying to me, "Give me your heart and I'll give you mine. I'll give you a new heart." It was sort of like my heart had been broken by losing my first husband and He wanted to heal it, and really did. I experienced a very deep healing which was a really profound spiritual experience for me. But there weren't any concrete answers, other than that, just that my heart was healed, that I was whole, and I had this heart that was Jesus' heart. How can you really love again with a broken heart? It was very shortly after I got back from Medjugorje that David came back into my life, like he said, as friends.

Whenever I thought about the idea of getting married again, I knew it would have to begin with friendship, and be built on that foundation. I just couldn't imagine getting into the dating scene and I couldn't imagine ever falling in love without it being based on mutual faith and trust and sharing of our deepest values. I began to realize what a precious and rare thing that is. All the men I knew were married or had taken a vow of celibacy.

When David came along, I was really glad to see him again, because we had been quite close as families. As you can imagine, we'd known each other as married to someone else, so of course I didn't fall in love with him back then. It really showed me how love is from God. When He wants to manifest what we call "falling in love,"

He can do it. But it's not the way it's often portrayed in movies, where these married people are so attracted to each other; they end up having an affair because they cannot resist it. I think that would really be 'falling in lust.' I think of falling in love as more like falling into God together, and allowing His love to be made manifest between us. It's still a very powerful attraction, as I was to find out.

David: Also, something occurred to me. The last year of Anna's life was a very intense time. So when Anna did pass away, I was really burned out. Anna died in February of 2003. So when I came up to our family cottage the following summer, in June, I was looking forward to just being in nature and resting. I wasn't in the mode of wife-hunting by any means. I just relished the thought of some down time. My children came up now and then through the summer, and so I had some good quality time with the children, good tears. Then in the summer of 2004, also at the cottage, the Lord just somehow chose that time for Posie and I to meet once again and begin our courtship.

Posie: David's daughter and my daughter are quite good friends, and their friendship started back at our retreat center when they were little girls. But over these years, with David's Ruth coming up to the area – my daughter Shanti lives in Killaloe – they just started seeing each other again and really hitting it off. I know on my daughter's part, the possibility of David and I coming together crossed her mind when she saw David hanging around in the area. As I said, I had been really praying and discerning whether I should stay in my house, since my children were growing up, and would be gone in a few years. So I thought perhaps I should fix it up and sell it, because if I was going to be a single person and maybe living some kind of a solitary life, that it might be wise to sell the house and move into something smaller. It needed quite a bit of fixing up. I took off time in the summer because the outside of the house needed painting, it needed new flooring, and the bathroom needed redoing.

My children in the area saw that it was a big job for me to

do this by myself. So they came to help with painting and started enlisting a few others to help too. David was one of the ones they thought of because he was at the cottage nearby, and he was always a very kind, caring person that would help anyone in need.

I thought, *Isn't that nice? He's feeling sorry for me and trying to help out.*

David: So to this day, I think there was a little bit of a conspiracy going on because Posie's son-in-law called me up and asked if I would lend a hand at Posie's house with the laying of some flooring. So I said, "Yeah, I have the time. I'd like to help." I came and that just gave me more contact with Posie, and that's what helped to kindle our first date and the period of getting to know one another better.

Posie: We had been doing the flooring and I'd been doing a little plumbing in the bathroom, cleaning out the sink traps, you know, one of the dirtiest jobs. It was on *this* day that he said, "Are you doing anything Friday night? Would you let me wine you and dine you?" I just about fell over. I was so shocked. I wasn't expecting that. He was just an old friend, like I said, feeling sorry for me. Maybe he *was* a little, too. (smile) Like, am I doing anything Friday night? I don't go out. I don't date. I stay at home with my kids. So it was a real shift, a *complete* shift in my life.

Like I said, I had felt that marriage was my vocation and I realize that God changes our vocation sometimes. But it had been such a strong call, and it didn't seem to be going away. I knew that if He did want me to be married again, it would be another beautiful love affair. It wouldn't be a marriage of convenience.

It's like something was transformed at that point. That's why I say it was like the Holy Spirit moving, because these thoughts were coming to me: *Wait a minute...I never experienced this...This is really strange...What am I feeling?* And it's funny because David's first wife and my first husband are the opposites of us. I'm the opposite of his wife, Anna and he is very, very different from my husband, Don. So it wasn't at all the same as my previous marriage. It was a very different thing. He had different good qualities that were endearing to me and that I loved about him. So I couldn't really compare it. We avoided a lot of the pitfalls that we were prone to in our first marriages, because they were just big lessons we learned about what *not* to do and how to be more tender and more patient.

David: Then too, we didn't have all the child-rearing responsibilities. It was a new period of our lives where we did have time to focus on each other more. Although Posie had two of her younger boys still living at home, they weren't small children.

Posie: There was one night. It was the Feast of the Assumption, which has always been a really powerful feast for me. He made me dinner. And there was something electric going on in the air, but we weren't really talking about that yet. Something unspoken was going on. I was trying to figure out if I was imagining it or not. But when I went home that night to my house, my mind was going around and around and I couldn't sleep. I think it was fairly early the next morning, I drove back to his cottage because I just had to talk to him. I just had to ask him. I don't remember exactly the words, but I was kind of blurting out and saying what I was feeling, that there's something going on. I figured I've got nothing to lose because if there isn't anything going on in his heart, then I'll just carry on the way I have been going, we'll be friends. But if there *is* something going on, then maybe we can talk about it. And I remember, I had gotten to the cottage and he was already out sitting by the water, and I walked down and I just spoke from my heart. I said, "It just seems like I'm falling in love with you and I don't know what to do and I just have to say that. Something's going on." And I don't remember what we said, really.

David: Neither do I.

Posie: I just remember thinking, *It's getting real now,* speaking from the heart, being vulnerable and yet not jumping to any conclusions, trying to do it gently. But then the topic was opened, and we started talking more about a relationship, and what was going on and yes, there was something happening and what is this? Neither of us had any other relationships since our spouses had died.

I remember one time, probably a few days after that, when we saw each other at Mass, I invited him over for brunch. We were sitting on the porch and he said, "Hmmm...That would be 14 children..." This was sort of the first time we started to talk about marriage. He was really genuine and sincere: "...how would we *do* that?" Then gradually, we talked more and more about it. We started to talk about marriage and what that meant, how it would happen and how it would impact our families, then we started talking about the timetable of it all. We didn't want to wait around too long. We knew how short life can be.

David: The times that we did have together, just sharing about the things of faith and family, it just became more and more clear. I don't know if I'm a typical guy. I don't know how much in touch I was, or I can't give it words very well right now, but it just grew. There was the realization that Posie would make such a wonderful companion in life and that our faith was so unifying. The rich background that our families had had, and that our Catholic faith was very important to both of us. In other words, we were on the same page. We were building something on rock, rather than the sandy soil of the world's values. It was a solid foundation.

So within the space of a few months, I formally proposed on October 1st, the feast of St. Thérèse. Then we were married that New Year's Eve of 2004.

In scheduling the date, we naturally wanted as many of our children to be there as possible so we picked a holiday time. Thirteen of our children were present at our wedding here in Combermere at our present parish, Holy Canadian Martyrs. It was even more beautiful too, because a number of the Madonna House community members were also able to be present. This community has been very important to both of our families. It was the talk of the village, "David and Posie are getting married!" To this day, people find such delight in the fact that our lives came together.

Posie: We wanted our wedding to be a big celebration. We knew that many people who are married for the second time have a quiet little wedding, sometimes even just in the sacristy. But we really wanted it to be a celebration of our love. We didn't have a lot of money to spend, so we had a potluck meal. We invited about 200 people, including our families and it was just a real, great time. There was nothing formal about it at all, but it was a real celebration and very joyful. In fact, some of the Madonna House people were here last night, talking about it, and how they just felt so filled with joy the whole evening.

David: Our children took part in the ceremony. We built into the service opportunities for them, especially bringing up the different gifts, and symbols that were important to us both. Many folks from the faith community that Anna and I had been part of in London, Ontario, were also present. That was such a great joy as well.

Posie: Once we knew this was love and this was forever, we didn't want to have an extended engagement because right or wrong, we knew how short life is and that you don't know how many years you have together. With our first marriages, we didn't know how many years we would have, or that they would be cut short. So we just wanted to make the most of every moment we had.   I can remember going through this pleading with God – I do this periodically with God – I try to bargain with Him. "Please God, do you think this time, *I* could die first? Because I don't want to go through this again." It's not like He yelled at me or I could hear His voice. But I got the distinct impression that He was saying, "Sorry, there's no deal. You must trust me to know the best time for each of you."

David and Posie (Rosalie) Douthwright live in Combermere, Ontario where they work for Madonna House Publications. As converts to the Catholic faith, Madonna House has been a source of inspiration and support for both of them for many years. David's first wife Anna died in 2003; Posie's husband, Don, in 1997. Married on the last day of 2004, they are now the proud parents to fourteen children, David's six and Posie's eight, as well as 22 grandchildren. David is usually quick to point out that he was an only child, proof of God's sense of humor. Both of their families first met in the early 80's at the Nazareth Catholic Family Retreat Centre run by Posie and her husband, Don McPhee, who also became a Deacon in the Catholic Church. Don and Posie's amazing story of conversion and journey home to the Catholic Church is recorded in a book, "Seekers of Truth - Finding the Faith" that Madonna House asked Posie to write. In addition she has written two other books for Madonna House Publications: "Marriage: A Fountain of Grace," of which David loves to say, "Yep, I thought it would be a good idea to marry the girl who wrote the book on marriage," and "Mothering: Becoming the Heart of the Home." In addition, she helped in the compiling of Christopher de Vinck's book, "Fathering: Building the New Civilization of Love." David and Posie attend Holy Canadian Martyrs Church, where they recently helped facilitate a Lenten-Easter reflection series on Pope John Paul's Theology of the Body as well as helping in the formation of the parish's pro-life group. They are also part of the marriage preparation team for the diocese.

David and Posie (and their combined families)
at their wedding in December 2004

Damon and Melanie Owens

Married April 24, 1993

The Longing to be Loved and Cherished

Damon and Melanie 1993

Damon: Our journey back to Christ began with what we now simply call "The Question," "Melanie, what if we stopped having sex?"

It's funny how different a question can be asked (or heard) with just a slight change of inflection. I intended to start an interesting conversation. Chastity had not been an issue of debate or even conversation between us, so I offered the question not as a proposal to stop but as a hypothetical-California graduate student-latte sipping-cosmic-what if. Neither of us had any idea what Our Lord had in store for us.

Though being from opposite coasts, we both grew up in similar Catholic families. We attended Mass regularly, went on retreats and participated in youth groups. At thirteen, I had a profound experience of God on an Antioch retreat that played a significant part in helping me remain chaste and drug-free through high school. Melanie's childhood memories are filled with songs from Catholic family summer camp and piling in the station wagon with seven brothers and sisters.

When we met as new graduate students at the University of California, though, we were both recovering from spiritually dark college years distant from God. During my undergraduate years at Brown, I partied, rarely attended Mass and, drawn by gospel choirs and organs, dabbled in other faiths.

Melanie: I had suffered in relationships during my college days at U.C. Santa Barbara, but continued to attend Mass regularly, though more out of habit than desire.

Damon: So, when we began dating, there was not much virtue, or even desire, left for us to draw on to be chaste.

Melanie "wowed" me the first moment I met her. What a smile! What a sweet soul! We could talk effortlessly for hours—and we did. I wanted to share everything with her. I wanted to know everything about her. I wanted to protect her. I wanted to love her, and I thought I did. Then, I asked . . . The Question.

Melanie, my new beloved, cried. I didn't know what was going on. *Is she hurt? Is she pregnant? Or, is she just emotionally unstable?* (I had not known her for that long!)

After ten inconsolable minutes, she simply said, "Yes."

Yes? Yes, what? Did she think that I was proposing we stop? Well, while my dulled conscience had been thinking our sexual "intimacy" was deepening our love, Melanie had been tortured with the reality that something was very wrong. When she tried to explain, it was as hard for me to hear as it was for her to speak.

Melanie: I knew Damon loved me, or at least was trying to love me, but sex made me feel used. Was he with me for me, or for sex? I had been afraid of bringing up the issue because I feared he would leave me for someone else. Now, after months of burying these fears, Damon brought up the subject and it was too much for me to bear.

Damon: So much for the cosmic "what if." After hours of tears, words and hugs, we made our decision to stop. For months, we struggled to stop on our own, and we continued to fail. We experienced the power of sex even in its misuse.

Melanie: I suggested that we speak to a priest for help.

Damon: Tough times, tough measures.

Melanie: We found a priest whose counsel would in time lead us to a redemptive understanding of sex, love, God and eventually marriage. Through counsel, confession, prayer and much struggle, we began a new, chaste relationship.

Damon: Chastity? Isn't that a fancy Catholic term for repressed sexual abstinence? That is what we both thought until we studied, prayed and began this struggle.

We discovered that true chastity flows from a sacrificial, and passionate, love. Without any theological or philosophical training, we worked on a redirection, reordering and reintegration of our sexual desire that would no longer hijack our love but serve it. We weren't looking to satisfy some abstract rule or article of faith, but simply to be happy. This just felt right.

I cannot overstate the difficulty of this struggle for both of us. But, far from hurting our relationship as we feared, chastity actually drew us closer than we ever thought possible. Our intimacy deepened, as well as our intimacy with God. The passion to be physical remained – and actually intensified – but we now had new vision and strength – and grace – to love, instead of simply seek self-satisfaction. We prayed together. We went to Confession.

We went to Mass. We received the Eucharist. We had to relearn how to love honestly.

Melanie: And, most affirming for us, I no longer felt used. I felt loved. I knew Damon was with me for me, and my dignity blossomed. We experienced the power of Love, real and true, and It began to heal us.

Damon: I remember once we were walking along the shores of Lake Merritt in Oakland and I reached out to hold her hand. As she pulled me close, I noticed she was crying and smiling.

Melanie: I knew he was holding my hand because he wanted to be close to me – not for sex or anything I could give, but for me!

Damon: After two-and-one-half years of chaste love, we married with such divine confidence (literally *con fide*: "with faith") only possible in a state of grace. Our struggle for virtue was neither in vain nor expired on our wedding day.

Though delivered, forgiven and redeemed as prodigals, we still work to overcome the damage of our pre-conversion sin. The chastity we lived as abstinence before our marriage is the chastity we live now as faithfulness within our marriage.

We look forward, by God's grace, to pouring all of His wisdom into the seven beautiful little girls and one little boy he has (so far) given us to train. As for them, may they be preserved from the brokenness that their parents experienced and be future witnesses of souls kept in purity.

Melanie and I have shared our story to over twelve thousand couples preparing for marriage. As NFP coordinators for the Archdiocese of Newark, we live, teach and promote Natural Family Planning* and Theology of the Body as a most excellent training to learn and grow marital love.

*For more information on Natural Family Planning, see Appendix at the back of the book.

Damon is the host of EWTN's "NFP: Embracing the Marital Gift." He and Melanie are co-founders of the New Jersey Natural Family Planning Association (njnfp.org). Damon is also founder of Joy-Filled Marriage NJ (www.joyfilledmarriagenj.com) and speaks nationally on marriage, NFP, Theology of the Body and Theology of the Family. Damon, Melanie and their family live in New Jersey.

The Owens Family

James and Ellen Hrkach

Married May 22, 1982

Please God, Send Me a Man

Ellen and James 1979

Ellen: I grew up in New Jersey and Philadelphia as a small child in the turbulent 60's and went through adolescence and my teenaged years in the 70's. Although we were Catholic, my family did not always practice the faith. Despite the fact that my parents and siblings had stopped attending Mass, I continued to attend church and to pray. Because I was very young looking, I did not date in high school or for the year or so afterwards. However, I longed to meet someone, that special person with whom I could spend the rest of my life. Every night I prayed, *Please God, send me a man.* I didn't specifically ask for a godly man, but I did ask for a good man. In fact, when many of my friends in high school were talking about what they wanted to do with their lives, I shared with them my deepest desire to marry a great guy and have lots of kids.

James: Born in rural Canada in the early 60's, it wasn't long before my family moved to the U.S.A. for work reasons and I was learning to deal with the heat of the Sunshine State. We stayed in Florida for six years and then left that world behind to return to Southeastern Ontario. All over again, I was introduced to snow and skating rinks and cold days that would take your breath away. I also became interested in music, buying my first drum set at the age of 13 and then not long after that, a guitar. I learned a lot from record albums, but most of my knowledge of music and performance was gleaned from music ministry at Mass every Sunday. In fact, most of my knowledge of life and love came from attending Mass as well. Like the majority of teenage boys, I wanted girls to like me, but was a little unsure of what to do once they did. Typically, I retreated into closets to have private conversations with my first girlfriend on the phone. I used to think this was because my family wouldn't understand our conversations or the meaning of our friendship. Now I see that it was because I didn't understand what our relationship was about...and I certainly wasn't comfortable having anyone monitor that situation.

Ellen: In response to this deep yearning to meet a wonderful guy and have lots of kids, I developed a crush on the teen idol, Shaun Cassidy, of TV's "Hardy Boys."

Also in response to this deep desire, and as a sort of distraction, I began to write to pen-pals from all over the world. At one point, I was writing regularly to over 100 people. One such pen-pal lived in Canada. I remember feeling quite a connection to her, even though we had only written letters to each other. We had a lot in common, not the least of which was a love for the "Hardy Boys." She eventually invited me up to Canada to visit her and her family.

During that visit, a few nights after I arrived, my pen-pal asked if I wanted to go with her to a jam session where her brother would be rehearsing with his rock band. I didn't particularly care for rock music, and I didn't really want to go, but I said yes to be polite. We arrived at the house and when I heard loud rock music, I immediately regretted my decision to be polite. We banged on the door and finally the music stopped and a young man came to the door and ushered us inside.

The band had evidently taken a break and most of the guys were standing around. One boy, however, was crouching, with his back toward me, a guitar in front of him, and he was playing the same three or four notes over and over again. I thought, *That fellow must be dedicated.* I also noticed that he had dark curly hair and bell bottoms (which were out of style at that time) which prompted me to think *He must not be too concerned about fashion.* A few moments later, the band members took up their instruments and the fellow with the dark curly hair turned around and began playing his guitar and singing. I know that it sounds cliché, but when I first saw his face, he was so handsome that he took my breath away. He played with such intensity that I couldn't stop staring at him.

James: Having let my first boy/girl experience dwindle to its logical end, I was a free man on the night Ellie and I met, not that I expected any new relationships anytime soon. I wasn't much for pursuit, except pursuit of excellence in music and art. That seemed so much easier to understand than girls. Ellie, on the other hand, was definitely in pursuit and had a hard time hiding it, even if she tried. One thing is for sure, though, her young looks were less intimidating for someone as shy as myself.

Ellen: Although I was 20 at the time, I looked more like 13 and was still rather immature. I didn't want to seem like I was coming on too strong, so I told my pen-pal's brother that I liked James and would love to go out with him while I was still in Canada. I was told that James was shy and usually quiet, but when we later met at a dance in the local curling club, we spent three hours talking outside (where it was less noisy). I was nervous because I liked him so much. I actually began the conversation by asking him a "conversation starter" that my pen-pal had given me in case I became nervous. "Nice trees around here," was all I could come up with. His answer really surprised me.

He said, "Yes, they are nice. I like the way the light is reflecting off the oak leaves over there." I never expected such a well-thought out and creative answer to a conversation starter. As we began to talk, I realized that he was indeed no ordinary young man. He was three years younger than me. Most girls my age would never have even considered going out with someone that much younger. But I saw in James a person who seemed much older, much wiser than myself. I liked him a lot, although I was not yet sure this was the person that God had sent me.

James: It's funny that although I would have gladly stood on a stage and produced a wall of loud noise to perform at any dance, I wasn't much for attending them. I certainly saw the empty meanings of much popular music, and spending time outside of the noisy dance hall was a definite option, especially when this time was to be spent getting to know a person from a different part of the continent, a girl, in fact, who seemed to want to get to know me. When time flies by so fast you can't keep track of it, you know you're having fun, and I certainly felt comfortable chatting with Ellie that night. So comfortable that I almost couldn't face the discomfort of having to see her return home.

Ellen: Later that week, when we said good bye to one another, I asked him if he would write to me. I realized that this would be a test of his character because he promised that he would write. So I arrived back in New Jersey and immediately wrote my first letter to James. I had already had the experience of writing to many pen-pals so I knew that I would be good at keeping in touch with him through letters.

In those days, we didn't have email or cheap long distance or texting, so he had to wait over a week before he received my letter. Then I had to wait two weeks before receiving a response. When I received his first letter, I knew he was the real thing. Over the next few months, he sent letters frequently and drew little pictures on the backs of envelopes or in the letters themselves, little pencil sketches of scenes, lions or the cartoon version of himself. On one particular envelope, he drew a man crawling over the desert, passing a glass labeled "H2O" and saying "Ellen, Ellen."

As we began to share thoughts and feelings over the next five months, I became more and more excited at the prospect that he was the person with whom I was meant to spend the rest of my life. I was fairly certain that he felt similarly because whenever he would sign his letters, he would write "Love, James," and underline the word "Love" in heavy black marker, although he never actually said the words "I love you."

James: I must admit, I wasn't much of a pen-pal and the only person I had ever or would ever write letters consistently to was Ellie. The delay between one writing and the other responding was frustrating, but it added a certain timeliness to my letters' content. I tended to write things that would matter regardless of when Ellie read them. One would wonder how different our conversation would have been otherwise...perhaps more focused on the smaller temporary issues of day-to-day life. One thing is for sure; Ellie's ceaseless and timely response to every letter I wrote definitely convinced me that there was someone who really cared about me, helping to cement my certainty that I was developing a relationship that was going to work. If she was putting aside the distractions of life just to make sure I got a response every few days, how much more would she truly be able to commit herself to being my lifelong partner when we were near each other?

Ellen: On returning to Canada just after Christmas 1979, when James and I were alone together, we pledged our love to one another and promised that, although we lived in different countries, that we would be faithful.

I was overjoyed because I had finally found the one I loved. Unfortunately, he lived 500 miles away. I had no idea what it would mean to carry on a long distance relationship for an unknown number of years. However, we were in love and it didn't seem to matter when we were together.

Although I was Catholic at the time – and had discovered that he was also Catholic – I figured that James was like most people who didn't follow everything that the Catholic Church taught. I wanted to give myself to him physically before I returned home from that visit so we would have something to hold us together. He was only 17 at the time, but he shared with me that he had always thought that he would wait until marriage to have sex. I was shocked that a 17 year old would turn down an opportunity like that, but in hindsight, his high ideals for morality and "pursuit for excellence in art and music" are the exact traits which attracted me to him in the first place.

We spent the rest of the week trying to enjoy the few days we had left together. When it came time to say goodbye, we both sobbed. Since we lived so far apart, neither of us knew when we would see each other again.

When I returned to New Jersey, I soon learned that having a long-distance romance was more painful than pleasurable. I wanted to be with him every moment, but that was impossible because we lived in different countries. In fact, it would be many months before we would be able to see each other again.

James: Telling someone that you love them and that you will be faithful over long distances and periods of time is a bit strange for a young rural kid, because it's like promising to be a hero. But the kind of focus and dedication that you feel when, amidst your troubled years, you think you've found true love, generates a load of confidence. Still, I needed frequent reminders that all of it was indeed real. With so little personal contact, you can begin to believe that you are imagining the relationship rather than actually living it. That's where letter writing, weekly phone calls and, even better, long taped audio cassettes really came through for us. There were no time pressures like those we felt while on the phone and there was an actual voice, unlike the letters.

Ellen: The tape idea was wonderful because it gave us an opportunity to hear each other's voices. We continued to call each other, but because long distance was so expensive back then, the calls were few and far between. Through these long taped messages, and through his continued letters, I was able to get to know James in a deeper, more profound way.

A year later, we decided that we wanted to become engaged. There was no official proposal from James, just an outpouring of my heart and soul, explaining to him that I needed to have a date, something to shoot for, a goal where we would be able to begin our life together. We decided on the date: May 22, 1982, which was a year and a half in the future. I would have time to graduate from college and work for a while, and James would be able to finish high school and the first year of university.

James: The timing had a definite practicality to it, but that didn't make it any less daunting for an 18-year-old boy who hadn't yet started his post-secondary education. I was, in fact, torn in various directions. I was an artist-type who rarely planned even one year ahead for anything, and yet I was convinced that I needed to start a life with Ellie as soon as possible. Then there was my own parents' separation which seemed to be inspiring in me a need for certainty that found one form of expression as I put the question to Ellie, "Are you sure you want to do this? Because when I get married, it will have to be for life because I will not put my kids through what I have been through." She answered yes, of course, but the fear of the unknown still played havoc with my mind as I tried to sort out the pro's and con's of the huge commitment I was making. As it turned out, I didn't have to wait until marriage to see that things weren't going to run smoothly all the time.

Ellen: About six weeks before we were married, I decided that I would bring up a rather awkward, but important, topic during one of our midnight phone calls (long distance was cheaper at that time). We had already discussed that we wanted to wait a while before having children because James had three years of university to finish and because we were both so young. We hadn't really talked much about how we would go about doing that, but I had always assumed that we would use contraception.

During the phone call, I said, "I've decided what I'm going to use to avoid pregnancy." James said, "Really? What?" I answered, "The diaphragm." He was silent for what seemed like an eternity, then finally said, "I had hoped that we wouldn't use birth control, Ellie." Then we launched into a rather heated discussion about contraception and something called "natural family planning" (NFP). The argument/debate went on for an additional month of letters, tapes and phone calls.

James: It may seem a bit strange for the 'guy' to be insisting on NFP, since it was going to require abstinence. However, one should be reminded here that I had these feelings not only because I was Catholic, but because I was quite artsy. My left-of-center thinking, however, was directed less towards the Church and more towards big industry. It seemed repugnant to me to invite a birth regulation company into the bedroom. I argued with Ellie about the beauty of natural/intimate sexual relations, not really understanding what the Church taught, but very much prepared to side with Catholicism when it came to an idealistic interpretation of sexuality.

Ellen: The conviction with which James spoke convinced me to trust him and to trust the Church. He said things like, "I don't want you putting something in your body which could hurt you," or "If you used a diaphragm, it would mean that you were holding back a part of yourself." I could tell that he didn't want to use contraception, not out of any selfish reasons but, on the contrary, for selfless reasons and in order to preserve the unity of our marriage. We eventually took an NFP class and a few years later, we became certified teachers of NFP.

We were married on May 22, 1982, in my hometown of Runnemede, New Jersey, with both Americans and Canadians helping us to celebrate. During the Nuptial Mass, James sang a song he wrote called "Forever Amen." We've now been married for 29 years and have five sons ages 12-24 (as well as seven babies in heaven.) When I prayed to God to "send me a man," He answered my prayer a thousand fold. Not only did He send me a man, He sent me someone who would continually challenge me (and us) to strive for holiness, and to embrace the joys and sufferings of married life.

James is an arts educator, artist, musician, recording engineer, stage actor, writer. He is the illustrator of the Shubert the Firefly children's books, and has been active in music ministry since the age of 14. Ellen is a freelance writer and award-winning author of two Catholic novels: Emily's Hope (www.emilyshope.com) and In Name Only (www.innameonly.ca). In Name Only received a Gold (First Place) medal in Religious Fiction in the 2010 IPPY Awards. Ellen blogs at http://ellengable.wordpress.com and writes monthly columns at Amazing Catechists and Catholic Mom. Together, James and Ellen create the Family Life cartoon for Family Foundations magazine. They have been active in marriage preparation since 1983, and have been a certified CCL/NFP teaching couple since 1984. They live in Pakenham, Ontario Canada.

The Hrkach Family

Mark and Kathy Cassanto

Married June 29, 1996

Finding True Love Through an Introduction Service

Mark and Kathy 1996

Mark: I returned to Canada after being away for three years and settled in Ottawa to have a year of discernment for the priesthood. The following summer, after working with Father Bob Bedard (founder of the Companions of the Cross) and Archbishop Marcel Gervais, that door closed. I had great apprehension about the direction my life would be taking.

Now that I wasn't pursuing the priesthood, I was looking for work. I landed a temporary job as a bingo caller. I had shift work and would sometimes work late into the night.

During this time, I committed myself to personal counseling. This was a pivotal time for me.

I thought of the spiritual direction I had received from Fr. Bob and Archbishop Gervais, and I now understood my strengths and weaknesses in a new light. More importantly, I was able to begin to come into my own. I was able to grieve some losses and accept things for what they were, with life-changing effects. It helped me to put my adult life and future hopes into perspective. At this point, I had a real desire for marriage that I felt was from the Lord.

I did not want to just date. I wanted to court someone in order to marry her. There was a real distinction there. In my younger years, I learned the difference between dating and courting. I really wanted to court the woman that God had chosen for me.

Lo and behold one day, in 1995, I got a piece of mail for an introduction service (introduction services were precursors to online dating services). It didn't appear to be a superficial matching process. I remember, there was a long Q&A with multiple choice that I completed and mailed back. About a month later, I got a phone call. I had an interview, and they offered me a membership, which included up to five introductions. I had two introductions by late autumn. It was a good feeling to meet someone, especially because they were screened and I felt that they had many things in common with me. When you are introduced to someone, you give yourself several dates to get to know each other with no pressure. This time of introduction is intended to help each other identify whether they want to pursue something more exclusive.

I received Kathy's details in November and I was the one to make the first contact. Kathy knew of me, as she was given my details as well. I seemed to always miss her in my attempts to reach her by phone and, unfortunately, she didn't own an answering machine. Finally, I decided to try at an hour that I hadn't tried before. It was about 12:30 a.m. and I woke Kathy up. I was very apologetic, calling at that hour, saying, "I really tried to reach you during the day." This was quite a first impression for Kathy.

Kathy: I was raised Pentecostal and had a strong faith. After post-secondary education, including a year in England doing a Masters, I had been unable to translate a career out of anything I had learned academically. I had been working for a year as a baker in a restaurant and working weekends a lot, so I wasn't going to church often, even though I was still faithful. When I got the flyer for the introduction service in the mail, I thought, *Yeah, what do I have to lose?* I had no concept of it actually working. I didn't think much of it until I got a call from them. It was July when I was interviewed, and they were very respectful and seemed genuinely helpful.

So I signed up then and chose a payment plan. I just didn't want to put too much money down at once and I only signed up for three contacts.

Time passed and I forgot about it for awhile. Then, at the end of November, a person from the agency gave me Mark's information. I remember writing it all down and they said, "Oh, he's a big teddy bear of a guy. The reason we're matching you up is, he's Catholic and we know you're Protestant, but you both score very high in our questionnaires on the importance of religion and family." So this gave me some trepidation. I didn't know what to think because I had been taught not to enter into a mixed marriage.

However, I said yes. As Mark said, we had a hard time getting the first connection, and we talked about three times on the phone. One of the best aspects of this introduction service was that there was no element of dating because we were both transparent about where we had been and what we wanted. Right from the beginning, Mark was sharing about his family and his faith journey and we found we had commonalities. We had both been to the same evangelical summer camp as kids. He definitely had had experiences of God, and witnessing the power of the Holy Spirit, and I was drawn to that.

Mark: As a cradle Catholic, I had been introduced to the Charismatic Movement when I was seven years old. Between eight and twelve, I had really good, memorable times of having Christ as someone very close to me. Then it became less important when I was a teenager. I had come through life's experiences of discerning my vocation, of university, of previous relationships, and ended up with the conviction in my heart, that the next step in my life would have more meaning than it had ever had before. In my early conversations with Kathy, I said something to the effect that "everything that I have done or touched, or tried to pursue has always failed." With Kathy, our relationship seemed to be the one thing that God was taking to fruition.

Our first date was December 1st, 1995. She picked me up at work and we went and saw a James Bond film. Then we had a drink at a local piano bar. I remember having a wine spritzer and feeling sophisticated. Although I rarely smoked, I had hidden away in my leather purse a pack of cigarettes. Had Kathy seen me take out a cigarette and light up – that wouldn't have gone over well on our first date. It is one of those things we laugh about now.

What I remember the most from the first date is that – myself more than Kathy – there was a lot of talking, a lot of sharing and it was all from the heart. There was trust building quickly. It was as if we were best friends; she was someone I felt privileged to be with and to share life with.

Kathy: Through all these dates, I was very overwhelmed at his presence, because he was always so excitable.

Mark: Extrovert, to the extreme.

Kathy: It was kind of funny because after the first date, I thought, *Oh man, I don't really know about this* and I looked back and saw that he had forgotten his winter gloves in my car. *Oh no, I have to see him again, at the very least, because I have to give him his gloves back.* I didn't know what to think because I hadn't had much experience with dating. So then the second date, we planned to go to a museum. When I arrived to pick him up, he was standing on the corner, frantically waving his arms.

Mark: (Laughing) And she was thinking, *Should I drive by and just keep going, or should I pick him up?*

Kathy: (Laughing) It was like he was trying to land an aircraft. (Pause) After that date he gave me "Rome Sweet Home" by Scott and Kimberly Hahn, which recounts their conversion to Catholicism.

Mark: By our third date, I knew that I had found the person I wanted to marry. That's kind of shocking, and it was something I didn't share with her until our fourth date. When I did share it with her, it was equally received. So that was really nice. At one point, I told Kathy that I was going to be traveling to visit my Mom in Baltimore at Christmas. About four or five days before Christmas, I asked Kathy to drive me to the airport. She returned the book to me. On the airplane I discovered that there was a letter inside it that stirred my heart. When I read Kathy's thoughts and feelings, how she felt about me so far, I was over the moon. It made me extremely excited and proud because I could share this with my Mom and family members.

Kathy: Within a couple days after receiving "Rome Sweet Home," I read it from cover to cover. Surprisingly, I didn't have any problems with the theology. I was also moved by the emotional vulnerability of the authors' conversions.

God had prepared me in a lot of ways by what I had seen, and what I had been learning about Catholics and about other Protestant religions along the way. The one thing that struck me was where the Hahns talk about purgatory, citing Hebrews 12:29, "God is a consuming fire." Though in God's mercy we will get to heaven through Christ's sacrifice on the cross, I could see that we would need further purification to be in God's holy presence in heaven. I remember lying in bed crying, because I knew that I wanted to become Catholic, but I just couldn't see how that was all going to work out. So I gave the book back to Mark with a letter and a photo of me for his trip out to see his Mom. On the way to the airport, I had my hand on the gear shift and he put his hand on mine and that was the first time I had ever held hands with anyone. I was overwhelmed because these experiences were all firsts. So we got to the airport and we said goodbye. He leaned over and kissed me, a chaste kiss, and I walked back to the car and I think I sobbed all the way home. That was a long ten days.

Mark: Yes, it was. The worst part of my visit was that I lost my purse. I left it on the roof of the car and it flew off when we started going. But with great relief, the local police picked it up and I got it back.

Kathy: I picked Mark up at the airport upon his return on New Year's Eve. I remember he said to me that the most important thing in the purse was my photo and letter. That was the right thing to say.

Mark: We stayed in watching Mr. Bean till midnight. I felt that one of the ways to truly express your fidelity, your love, is a real good kiss, a nice kiss. I gave her a chaste kiss but a little more meaningful than a peck. That was another first for Kathy. Kathy's reaction was emotional, but in a good way.

Because of my enthusiasm for the Catholic faith, I was taking on the burden to try to have all the answers, and influence what God was doing in Kathy's life on a spiritual level. This started to create friction between us.

Kathy: Because I didn't want to hear it from him.

Mark: One day, I had come home from work, and we were on the phone. Kathy spelled it out for me how she felt. Then there was silence because I was really listening. I felt the Holy Spirit at work telling me to give it over to the Lord. The Holy Spirit had a very clear message, saying, *She is My daughter, she is Mine, leave her with Me, trust Me.* I'm glad that happened because God changes hearts, not me.

Later, I realized Kathy's witness had made me appreciate the treasure of the Church I had taken for granted.

We were having a whirlwind relationship, but something was still missing. I needed to confirm my desire to enter into a covenant.

On February 1st, Kathy and I were together at her place and I got down on my knee. I said, "I really need to ask you to marry me." And she said yes.

So in this time of preparing for marriage, Kathy felt quite good about things. Kathy felt ready to commit to coming into the Church. The pastor counseled her not to rush and she decided to wait for the RCIA (Rite of Christian Initiation for Adults) program the following year.

Kathy: I can sum up by saying my journey to becoming Catholic is inextricably linked to my courtship with Mark. But there's also an element that I became Catholic in spite of him and not because of him. The general stereotype is if you marry someone from another religion, you convert to their religion because it's the cultural thing to do, but that was the opposite of how I felt.

Mark: Kathy's journey to the Church brought insights, and her own thirst for knowledge for the faith, which far exceeded mine.

During this time, I began doubting, feeling stressed, and not praying. As a result, the enemy had open access to my emotions. I had a haunting feeling in the back of my mind – about everything I've ever committed to doing, never fully followed through, never coming to fruition. But then I realized that God's hand had opened and closed the doors of my life. I received good counsel through a friend that I take myself "too seriously. Lighten up!"

Kathy: Something had happened to me a couple years before this, when I had been doing my Masters in England. While attending an Evangelical Church, a missionary spoke about being open to thinking outside the box where you should go in life, including going to other countries to proclaim the Gospel. Although I had been exposed to a lot of missionary activity, I had never felt an interest.

However, one of things he talked about, and which struck my heart so deeply was when he was talking about Genesis 12, when Abraham gets his call from the Lord and His promise to make a great nation out of him. His amplified version of Genesis 12:1, said, "Go away for your own reasons, from your country and from your kinfolk." The missionary had printed the verse onto bookmarks, one of which I had carried around with me for years without understanding what it meant.

Mark: I invited Kathy to attend Mass with me that she never took up initially.

Kathy: I was working every weekend so I couldn't join him at first. Finally I decided to attend Saturday night Mass at Mark's parish during Lent. As soon as Mass started, I was moved by the foreignness of the liturgy. It was all very reverent and beautiful, but outside of my experience. Then, the first reading came. It was Genesis 12:1-4, the verses I had been given three years before. I felt the Lord's touch which brought both blessing and emotional upheaval.

Meanwhile, I agreed in theory with a lot of the theology of Catholicism. Nothing was bothering me. I understood the papacy. I understood the basic precepts of Marian theology. These were not stumbling blocks for me.

Mark: We also had an opportunity to drive to Baltimore together for Kathy to meet my mom.

Kathy: It was a break of routine for me. I stayed with Mark's mom, and Mark stayed at his grandmother's condo and it was great. Mark's mom was so gracious.

An issue I dealt with was the lack of support from my side, particularly friends from Bible college who were against me marrying a Catholic. They couldn't understand what my attraction would be first of all, to the Catholic Church and then secondly, to Mark. So I was often second guessing myself and pulling back. I know there was one point during the trip where, I think I tested him, saying, "Why do we have to get married in the Catholic Church? That was before we had our marriage prep course. So it was kind of an uneven balance of everybody on Mark's side encouraging me, and everybody on my side being very cautious. And yet we pressed ahead.

Mark: Kathy and I decided to receive some counseling from the person who had helped me previously.   One of the things we learned was to live our lives together being 100 percent responsible for 50 percent of our relationship. Again, this goes back to the Lord's word to my heart, about backing off. It's really, really hard to trust, to let it go. But I realized that God gave us a pearl of great price.

Kathy: The counselor said that Mark had a tendency to take over all the relationship and my tendency was to pull back and not take responsibility for any of the relationship. Learning this allowed me to be more active and vocal in making decisions.

Mark: Now everything started coming together. We took the marriage preparation course at my parish. The talk on Natural Family Planning (NFP) only confirmed my desire to be open to life. Being an only child, God only knows how I formed my conscience about NFP. NFP was never this *should we, shouldn't we*; it was just there. We just had to learn what to do.

Kathy: I had been exposed to Protestant families who were very providentialist and open to large families. With my scientific background, I was predisposed to avoiding the use of artificial contraceptives. I soon grew to appreciate the wisdom of the Church's teaching on openness to life and NFP.

Mark: It was difficult to have self control during the latter part of our courtship, but by God's grace we remained chaste. This added something very beautiful to our marriage.

Kathy: All through this process, prayer and Scripture were important. Verses like in 2nd Timothy 1:7 were especially relevant, where it says "God has not given us a spirit of fear but of love, power and a sound mind."

After the rehearsal dinner, Mark and I hardly had a chance to say goodbye. I got home and I woke up at 4:00 a.m. The phone was blinking because Mark had left a message. He said, "We left each other so quickly tonight..." and he recorded a prayer for the wedding day, that everything in the service would glorify God and inspire other people to see our true relationship with Christ.

Mark: And I guess the only thing to add was that when I saw Kathy and I held her hand at the altar, it wasn't this nervousness of doubt. It was, *I can't believe I'm actually here.* In the church photos, I can see the joy of the sacramental graces in our expressions.

Kathy: We didn't have a Mass in the ceremony out of respect for my side of the family. But in that moment of saying our vows, at least for myself, it was like there was something beyond me or inside of me lifting me up to say these words that it wasn't just me saying them. I just remember that. After that, if there was any time when it was hard in our marriage, there was no way that I could say that I didn't say those vows with a free, total, faithful, fruitful commitment. In that moment, I knew what I was doing, and that God was giving me the grace to fulfill my promise to Mark.

That following Easter, at nine months pregnant, I was received into the Church.

Mark: We have now been married for 15 years and have had nine children: three angels in heaven and six beautiful children with us: Anne (14), John Paul (12), Eunice (11), Daniel (9), Maria (6) and Joseph (3).

Mark is a computer specialist and runs his own business (www.clickintherightdirection.com). Kathy runs a home-based baking business (www.theywontkeep.com) and is a homeschooling mom of six. They are an NFP promoter couple for the Couple to Couple League. The Cassanto Family (along with Mark's mom, Regina) live in Braeside, Ontario.

The Cassanto Family (with Mark's Mom, Regina)

Leon and Mary Lou DuBois

Married November 29, 1952

Novena to Marry the Right Girl

Lee and Mary Lou 1952

Lee: I was overseas in the Navy and I had prayed a novena on board, and the intention of the novena was that I would marry the right girl. Of course, I had been going around with a girl for more than four years. Normally, I would get letters from her. At the bottom, it would always say, "All my love, Your Peggy." I did get a Christmas card, and when it finally came sometime in January, it said "Peggy." So I figured there was something wrong.

When I returned home, I called her and I said, "Is this what I think it is?" She said, "Yes." As it turned out, her father told her that now that I'm in the Navy, sailors can't be trusted.

For some reason, I wasn't all broken up about this. I had called two girls to go out and neither one of them would go out with me because they figured, "He's going with Peggy."

John, my best friend, went around with Mary Lou's best friend, Helen. We were going to go out on a double date and I said, "I can't get anybody to go out with me." John said, "I'll take care of that."

I didn't have a car, but he did, and so they came around to my house to pick me up. When I opened the door, who was in the back seat but this good looking girl, and that's what attracted me. I don't know, we just hit it right off. She was going with somebody else at the time. I told her that I had to go back overseas again and said, "Don't do anything until I come home." So when I came home, we got together.

Mary Lou: I knew about Lee from all the dances we went to. Back when I was a freshman; he was a senior and he always won all the jitterbug contests. He was so handsome. I never thought that I would have a date with him. At the time Lee and I met, I was actually engaged to another fellow and I had accepted the ring.

Helen called me and she said, "You remember Leon DuBois? He doesn't have a date. He's only home for a few days. Could you break your date?" So I broke my date and they picked me up.

He didn't have the sailor suit on; he had this navy blue pinstripe suit with a white shirt and I thought, *Oh, he's so handsome.* Everybody in that group was so funny. We just laughed all the time. So I said, "Where are we going?" They said, "We're going to go over to New Jersey." There were all these clubs where you can have a drink and we all loved to sing and dance, so they ordered me a Brandy Alexander, and I had quite a few of them. We got up on the stage and we sang, "Aba Daba Honeymoon."

The next day, I said to my girlfriend, "I'm so sick. It's a good thing my mother isn't home," because I would have been grounded for ten years. (My mother was in Florida and my father was looking after us. He was a sound sleeper and didn't know what time I came home.)

So my friend said that Lee had to go back soon. Lee called me up the next day and I thought, *Well, come on over.* So the big thing back then for going on a date was the movies and the ice cream parlor. Again, he came in his navy blue suit and we talked about the fun we had and we used to sit on the sofa before he went back overseas and we would talk. We had the music on, just talk, talk, talk, lots of kissing, but nothing else, just kissing and talking.

Lee was getting ready to go back overseas, so I asked my mother if he could stay until 12 or 1:00 since I wasn't going to see him for six months. So she said "All right." After she went upstairs, we turned a light off and more hugging and kissing and music and talking.

Our romance, really our courtship, was mostly by mail because he was away for six months. We started writing back and forth. I have every single letter he ever wrote. We used to do a poem together. I would write a line and the next letter, he would write a line. After we moved, I said to his mother, "Where are all the letters that I wrote to Lee?" She said, "I threw them away." I was so disappointed. But every now and then I'll pull one of his letters out and I'll read it to him, and he'll say, "Oh, I didn't write that."

Lee: One of the things that I think was really great was when we got engaged. We got engaged in the 69th Street Terminal in Philadelphia. We were waiting for the train. I got down on my knee, and I proposed to her and I gave her an engagement ring.

We went down the shore with Helen and John. We went out that night and I said, "I'm going to take Mary back to her apartment. Hold off for a while," because I figured I was going to put a move on her. The only thing was when I did, she jumped up and took the ring off and threw it out the window.

Mary Lou: It's funny, though, being brought up in a Catholic school back then, you had this fear of doing something wrong. The fellow that I was engaged to before Lee, he was in the Army, and my mother let me go down on the bus to Norfolk for the weekend. I don't think I would have let my daughter do that and my mother was basically very strict. So, I guess, she trusted me. And she trusted the fellow too. I was in a hotel all by myself. I said to him, "Can you spend the night and sleep on the floor? I'm really afraid to stay here."

"No." He said, "People will think the worst." So back then, it was so different than it is today.

Lee: In 1947, girls didn't put out. Or at least I didn't know any of them.

Mary Lou: When Lee came out of the service, my mother didn't want us to get married until the following year in the warmer months.

He said, "Why do we have to wait so long?" So we picked Thanksgiving weekend in November of 1952, and she was horrified. As it turned out, all the fellows that he was in the service with came. Since he was working with United Airlines, we had our choice of going half-price either to Bermuda or Aspen, Colorado. So we chose Bermuda.

The other thing is that we had no sex education. The night before I was married, I said to my mother, "We have to have a talk." And she said, "About what?" I said, "I don't know what to do." Do you know what my sex talk was? "Don't worry. Lee's in the Navy; he'll know what to do." That was my sex education.

So we went away on our honeymoon.

Now, I had never gotten undressed in front of anybody, even my sister and I never got undressed in front of each other. I had lots of these gorgeous nightgowns. I'd go into the bathroom and put this gorgeous nightgown on, turn the light out and come out. After about four nights, Lee said, "Am I ever going to see any of these nightgowns?" Of course, nowadays, kids have less inhibitions.

Lee: When we left Philly by train to go to New York to catch a flight to Bermuda, we were on the train in our matching grey suits. Even the luggage was gray and she had a corsage and everybody was looking at us. And the next morning we wake up, it's a major snow storm.

Mary Lou: It was an old prop plane. While we were in Bermuda, we met a couple from New York and they had been married the same time as we were, and she said, "We're cashing our ticket in and taking the boat back." I said, "I don't want to get back on that plane." It was worse going back.

Lee: When we got back to the terminal in New York, I had 75 cents.

Mary Lou: It bought us a ham sandwich and two cups of coffee. Times were really tough. Everybody in our era just got married. They didn't say, "Does your husband have a new job?" We were all so in love and we all got pregnant right away. The only thing that kept us together was that we loved one another.

Of course, we could talk about anything and Lee was very funny. We laughed all the time and he seemed like a responsible person. He was kind. My mother always said, "You can judge a man by how he treats his mother," and Lee adored his mother. I saw the comradery with him, like when I first went to his house, he would go in and hug his mother and kiss her and he'd say, "let's dance" and stuff like that. That, and talking on the telephone. We just had so much in common. We loved going to the movies.

Lee: That's the same today. That has never changed. We get up in the morning and we sit at the breakfast table and we can talk. It's never one of these things where you just sit there and look at each other. I don't know what it is. There's just always a topic.

Mary Lou: We do have different interests. He golfs and I don't. And we have separate friends, but basically, we still enjoy one another's company.

Lee: I turned 81 in January, so people have asked me, "What would you say has helped you with your longevity? I believe the most important thing is to have a sense of humor and to be able to laugh at yourself. A sense of humor is so primary because people don't realize what effect it has on your metabolism. If I start thinking, I'm old and don't have a sense of humor, I'm going to sit here like this, that's not the way it should be. I believe this is one of the things that has helped us, that we have a sense of humor and being able to laugh at ourselves.

Now, my father wasn't a big churchgoer, just my mother. But here's the thing. Back then, if you went to a Catholic school through grade school, you had to go to Mass. There were no ifs, ands or buts and they took attendance. In high school, the church paid your tuition. And they would also take attendance. Now, if you didn't go to Mass, the priest would come to your house and say, "Do you want to pay your tuition yourself? No? Then make sure your son starts going to church on Sunday."

Mary Lou: You wouldn't think of not going to church. And even if we were away on holiday, we used to go down to the seashore and the first thing Sunday morning, we went to Church. And we always went to daily Mass during Lent. We used to take the subway to go to Mass.

Lee: Even when I was in the Navy, they had a Mass, when I was aboard ship, it would be jammed with people.

Mary Lou: Anyway, not only do you have to love the person, you have to like them. A lot of people are madly in love. After you're married and all that glitter wears off, you have to like the person.

Lee: Like Mary Lou says, love is one thing, but you have to genuinely like each other, and that's really paramount.

Lee is a retired Boeing specialist and Mary Lou is a full-time homemaker. They have three grown sons, five grandchildren and two great-grandchildren. They are originally from the Philadelphia area, but now live in Arnprior, Ontario, Canada. They have been married for 58 years.

Lee and Mary Lou DuBois

Mark and Yvette Bourque

Married May 15, 1993

A Friendly Wager

Mark and Yvette 1991

Yvette: Before Mark and I met in 1991, I had noticed him in high school. I thought he was a very good looking guy, although I had never gotten to know him. A couple of years went by. Mark was going to college in Peterborough (three hours away) and I was going to college in Pembroke. He was coming home on the weekends because his family lives here in Petawawa and I would still see him occasionally. At this point in my life, my mom had just died a month before we actually met.

When I was growing up, we never went to church, but

several of my friends knew Mark. They told me that he goes to church every Sunday, no matter how late he was out on Saturday night. I was intrigued by that, even though I didn't understand why somebody would go to church when they were tired.

One night, a group of girls and I were at a dance bar and Mark was there with his friends. Mark had asked me to dance a couple of times, so we got to know each other a little bit.

Mark: I was attracted to Yvette's curly dark hair as it was long and big and attractive. The more I got to know her, the more I realized that she was a smart, fun and happy person, the kind of person that I wanted to be with all the time. She has a beautiful smile and is a beautiful woman. We started off as friends. I had a friend who really liked her and I didn't want to intrude on his infatuation, but at the same time, once I knew she wasn't interested in him, I wanted to continue our relationship.

Yvette: Mark told me that his friend was interested in me, but I wasn't interested in his friend at all. One night Mark and the two guys he lived with were having a dinner party, so he invited me and several other people to come over. While we were talking, I got the idea that I'd like to invite him to my nursing graduation.

Mark: When she invited me to her graduation, I thought, *This is great!* I got to meet her dad and her family. It was just like everything fell into place.

Yvette: Mark was more of a gentleman than I had been used to dating, so we had a very good time.

Right after my nursing graduation, I went away to Bermuda for seven days. I didn't see him for a week, but many times while I was in Bermuda, I was thinking that I would like to be back home, to be with Mark.

When we got back, I bumped into him again late one night

at a local restaurant/bar. I teased and challenged him by saying, "There's no way you're going to make it to church tomorrow because it's really late and I doubt you're going to be able to get up."

He said, "Oh, yes I will. I'll be at church tomorrow." So we had this little bet, this friendly wager, going.

I said, "How will I know you made it to church?"

He said, "Well, do you want to come?"

I said, "Are you inviting me?"

He said, "Yeah, but you probably won't make it either. You're never going to get up that early. I go to church at nine."

I said, "Okay. We'll see. I'll be there."

I am a bit stubborn. If I make a bet with somebody, I don't like to lose. So I set my alarm clock. I got up and I met him at the door of his house. He was just walking out to his car. Of course, he was shocked that I was there, and I was surprised that he was awake too. So I followed him to church.

I hadn't been to church in years so I didn't know when to stand, sit or kneel. I didn't know any of the responses, except the Our Father. Several of the pews were taken up by his family members (he's from a large family of 11 kids). After church, we went back to his parents' house because every Sunday involves brunch at his mom and dad's. So I met his family. I was attracted to the fact that he was very committed to his faith and to his church. I had never met a guy that went to church, let alone, of his own free will, without being forced to go by his parents.

Mark: The invitation to church was one of our first dates. At the time, I was praying for a spouse, for a lifelong partner. I had dated other women, but it just didn't seem like there were any sparks there or anything that jumped out at me like – this is the one – until I met Yvette. When that happened, I knew my prayers had been answered.

As Yvette said, her mom had just died before we met. She had Lou Gehrig's Disease, so Yvette carried a lot of family responsibility between going to school and looking after her mother. Her mother was in the hospital in Peterborough, so Yvette wasn't around much because she spent most of her time visiting her mom. At that point, I wasn't around either. I was living in Peterborough and I had just moved back to Petawawa.

So this all began very shortly after her mom passed away. When you think about it, it might have been a coincidence, but the way I looked at it, I was praying to God and saying, *Enough of this single life. I don't need this anymore. I need somebody to share my life with.* I was thinking about raising a family and having all the wonderful things my parents had. This is how I grew up, so my prayers were answered.

Yvette: At the time, I wasn't praying for anything. When my mom died, my cousin spent some time with my mom just before she passed away. The nursing home was three hours away so my family could only visit on the weekends.

About four days before my mom died, my cousin, Linda, was with her. Linda used to visit frequently to read books and her mail to her. Since my mom had Lou Gehrig's Disease, she couldn't talk and she hadn't said anything in years. Her neck muscles were very weak, so in order for her to sit up, her neck would have to be all the way back, staring up at the ceiling. On this one particular night, Linda heard my mom say, "I'm tired and I really want to go." My mother hadn't spoken in over four years so this was really incredible. My cousin said to my mom, "Don't worry, Yvonne. If you need to go, everyone will be okay...you go ahead." My mom waited until we visited her on Friday. Later that night, she passed away. Linda told me that she had wanted to share this with the family, but she didn't want us to think she was crazy. I believed her when she shared this experience. I thought, *Oh, I believe those things are possible.* Then within a month, I met Mark. It wasn't until a year later, maybe a year and a half, I could look back and say, "I think there was some kind of an exchange here." My mom had to die. She wasn't going to live forever with Lou Gehrig's Disease, because there's no cure. Now Mark was in my life, somebody who went to church, and I'd never known anybody like that before. It seemed like a God-incident.

My mom died at the end of February. It wasn't until the summertime when I wanted to take a trip back to Peterborough where my mom was buried. My mom's headstone hadn't been put in yet since it was winter and they only do that in the summer. Mark came with me and, to make a long story short, we got into a really big fight that weekend, our only fight up to that point. At the time, I was not a very forgiving person to anyone outside my family.

Mark: The fight was totally my fault, by the way.

Yvette: So I had given him the silent treatment for a few days and didn't call him. He called me and I wasn't very talkative. Finally, he said, "I'm coming over."

Now, my mom's favorite bird was a blue jay and we had this engraved on her headstone along with a few other things. So Mark was apologizing for this bad weekend, and he said that something very strange happened to him, and I said, "Oh yeah?"

Mark: I was driving the work truck that day, not paying close attention, and this blue jay flew right in front of the truck and shocked me, surprised the heck out of me. I had this sense that it was a sign from Yvette's mom, or maybe God, saying, "Wake up and don't miss this opportunity!"

Yvette: So there were these little spiritual events that opened my eyes along the way. I knew that Mark's faith was important to him, and I certainly wasn't going to be someone who kept him from going to church. I didn't understand it yet or what exactly the attraction was, but I noticed that Mark's family was different than my family and in a good way. He was one of 11 children, so I wondered, *What's behind this big huge family? Why would they have so many kids? What a sacrifice this must be for his mom especially.*

I had dated a number of different guys and I could identify quickly what I didn't like about them. I didn't really know what I wanted in a guy, but I knew what I didn't want. Those guys didn't last long, because once I realized they were not the one, I didn't want to be bothered continuing it. So when I met Mark, I didn't have any feelings of, *Oh, this is not what I want.* I had many more feelings of *Oh, this is very good. This is very different. This is more like it,* even though I didn't know exactly what that was. It just felt right. We got along very well. He was a real gentleman. For me, I looked at a lot of things, like, would he be a good father? Of course, he had a big family and he's been around many babies. Would he be a good husband? Did his friends respect him? Everything just fit and everything was a yes.

Mark: As Yvette said, I am one of 11 children. With regard to how I treated women in general, I have three older sisters and I was brought up to respect them. And, of course, they also had a lot of advice for me when I was dating.

As well, I had a strong Catholic upbringing. I learned to trust God, to respect others. And I was especially close to my mom. I had a great deal of respect for her.

Yvette: You can tell a lot about a fellow by how he treats his mother, and Mark always honored and respected her.

Mark: I was also brought up to honor Mary, the mother of Jesus. My family held her in high regard and the Rosary was a big part of our family life. My parents always said that if you need a job or if you need anything, pray the Rosary.

Yvette: Since meeting Mark I was just beginning to learn about my Catholic faith. I asked a lot of questions and was getting answers from people who would know. So I was growing in my faith, although I can't say that it was strong enough at that time that I understood the importance or the meaning of a Catholic wedding. I just knew that it would have to be a Catholic wedding because we're both Catholic and Mark would want that without question.

Once we started regularly dating and I was frequently around Mark's family, especially on Sundays after Mass, it was my time to ask questions and get answers. I was very open to whatever I was told. Mark's dad was very knowledgeable about the Catholic faith because he had an answer to every question. He's read a lot of books and he's passed a lot of books and DVDs regarding the faith my way. I felt that because I was born a Catholic, I should know what it means to be a Catholic.

I received it all very easily. I understood the Catholic Church's teaching, although I found some of it hard to live. It all made sense, why God wants us to live this way and why we have these commandments and why we receive communion every week (at a minimum) and why we need the Sacrament of Reconciliation.

So I grew very quickly in my faith. I was a big sponge and took it all in and this was a pretty surprising and positive thing for Mark. He was excited that I was moving right along in the faith area.

Now, my biggest example, if I could say, for living this faith was Mark's mom and dad, their trust and their joy and their servant mentality: just give, give, give and never thinking about what they're receiving back from any of their kids. I thought, *Wow, I'd like to be like that, even a little bit.*

Mark: I felt called to sacramental marriage with Yvette because I had found my lifelong partner. It was chemistry. I just knew that she was the one, and I wouldn't have gotten married any other way than in the Church with God involved because that's the way I was raised. If she didn't want that, then it probably would have been very difficult for me, because God has to come first.

We dated for a year, we got engaged and we were married a year later.

Besides the one incident (and that happened at the beginning), there were no other difficulties. We were in love and there was no need to wait. We just wanted to be married.

Yvette: When Mark made that bet with me many years ago, it took me on an unexpected journey of faith and love. We're both thankful to God for bringing us together.

Mark and Yvette live in Petawawa, Ontario. Mark works as an electrician/fire alarm technician. Yvette works as the Director of Youth Ministry for the Diocese of Pembroke. They have been married for 18 years and have four children ages four months to 17.

The Bourque Family

Chris and Micki Williams*

Married September 16, 1995

An Incredibly High Ideal

Chris and Micki 1995

Micki: We were introduced by mutual friends, a married couple, in November of '93. I knew the couple from law school. The year after graduation, I came up to Michigan to visit with them; while I was in one room talking to the wife, the husband went in the other room and called Chris. He told him they had a friend visiting for the weekend, she's single, she's Catholic, and she's not seeing anybody. Would you like to meet her? Chris said, "Well, I've got nothing better to do this weekend, I guess so." He didn't know too many people in Michigan at that point, so the couple was trying to get him out to meet some people.

The next night, those friends and I had planned to go to dinner with some other friends who'd recently graduated from law school. There was one seat left at the table when Chris got there, and it happened to be right across from me. Of course, I didn't see any of this coming, because they didn't bother to inform me that they were setting it up. If I had known, I would have refused to go, because I was quite happy being single at that point and life was good.

At any rate, we chatted all through dinner. Afterwards, he came back to the house with our mutual friends and me. I was sick that day, so I wasn't in the best frame of mind, and I ended up getting the impression that he was a sort of pompous, arrogant, self-absorbed jerk, which totally isn't Chris at all. I thought he was argumentative because he liked to have discussions and tried to play devil's advocate. I was really annoyed. He stayed till 12:30 a.m. I kept wishing he would leave, so I could go to bed.

Chris: I thought she was staying up because she was so enthralled in the conversation.

Micki: I'll talk to anybody. I'll even talk to people I don't like just because I'm a talker. I didn't like him, but I found several things interesting. Our favorite football team growing up was the Dallas Cowboys and each of us had the Cowboys' quarterback, Roger Staubach, as our favorite athlete, so I thought that was kind of cool. I found out that Chris was politically conservative, which I also thought was very cool. However, all that together still didn't take away from the fact that I really didn't like him and I wanted him to go away.

As he was getting ready to leave that night, he asked me if I had a business card. I was a lawyer, and lawyers are all about networking, so I started handing him my card. Before it was out of my hands, he said, "Do you have a home number you can write on that?" Immediately what went through my head was, *Who does this guy think he is, asking me for my home number? I don't even like this guy. But I can't be mean and tell him he can't have my card now. And I'm certainly not giving him my home number.* So, as politely as possible, I wrote my direct dial number at my office on that and said, "Here's my direct dial." But as I was giving him my card, I was actually praying, *Dear God, please don't let this guy call.*

Chris: I got the completely wrong impression. She was so polite, I didn't get the signal at all that she wasn't interested. All I knew is that she was young, Catholic, and conservative and I'd had so much trouble meeting anybody like that. I thoroughly enjoyed our conversation, so I totally misread that first day.

But here's what struck me most about her. We were sitting at our mutual friends' house, talking about courtship and marriage. Somehow or another, she said that she wouldn't marry someone who didn't love her enough to save himself for her even before they met. He absolutely had to be a virgin. That struck me as an incredibly high ideal. But also – and I think this is why she thought I was argumentative and pompous – I got a little bit defensive about what she was saying. When I was younger, and wasn't very well-formed religiously, I came close to falling in that area, and not saving myself for the girl I'd eventually marry. But I see now that the grace of God preserved me in that. So I was argumentative because I wanted to defend myself and where I had been when I was younger. That's why I posed so many questions like, "What if somebody only fell once, and it was many years ago, and they really regret it now, and they repented of it and never did it again?" She kept insisting that no, that still wasn't acceptable for her. The person had to have saved himself for her.

Micki: I explained that I could still be friends with that person. I wouldn't judge that person. We could still be best buds for life. But I wouldn't marry that person, because he hadn't loved me enough to wait for me.

Chris: My first thought was *Good luck with that.* Her ideals seemed too high, and she didn't seem at all flexible. After I had left, and I had the chance to reflect, I became inspired by what she had said. Partly, it was because I realized, *Hey! I still do qualify!* and that this is a woman who is a pearl of extremely high price. She knows that she's worth a lot (and not in an arrogant type of way). She knows her value and her dignity, and she's not going to allow herself to be bought cheaply. She wasn't going to be given away to just any guy who came along.

I concluded that Micki was a person who was worth striving to get to know, and I wanted to see if something could really happen with her. That was why I was so dogged in calling her, and why I continued to call for a month. It helped that she didn't let on that she wasn't interested. So I thought, *Wow, she keeps taking my calls. She keeps staying on the phone with me for an hour and a half. She must really be interested in me.* Of course, she wasn't, but I didn't know that. That's what kept me going through that month or whatever it was before we actually got together for our first date.

Micki: I should explain a little more why I said what I did about not marrying someone who hadn't loved me enough to wait for me. Something happened when I was 16, just kind of by happenstance. I was laying in bed one night, and I just prayed (and I'm sure it was the grace of God that inspired me to pray this), *Dear God, please help me to save myself for the man that I'm going to marry, and please help me to wait for marriage.* That simple prayer kept me out of a lot of trouble as I got older and went through life. When I was in college, someone had said, "Start praying now for whomever it is you're going to marry." So, probably freshman or sophomore year, I started praying, *Dear God, please bless whoever it is you have for me to marry.* And I might have even added, *Please help him to love me enough, even now, to save himself for me, even though he doesn't know me yet.*

When Chris started calling, I tried to find a way to gently tip him off that I wanted him to stop calling. I kept dropping these little hints trying to scare him off. Like, "I've already got my wedding dress, because it was on sale 75 percent off when I was a second year law student, and I couldn't pass that up." But he said, "Wow, what does it look like?"

Chris: She's thrifty.

Micki: *Rats, that didn't work.* So the next phone conversation, I said, "My dad has hated every guy I've ever dated." He said, "You just haven't brought the right guy home yet." *Darn, that didn't work either.*

Chris: I had encountered fathers much worse. I was confident that I could handle anything her dad could throw at me.

Micki: But I thought my ace in the hole was, "When I get married, I want to have four kids." I was a Protestant at the time, so four kids seemed like a whole lot of children. He said to me, "What? Only four?" I said, "How many kids do you want to have when you get married?" He said, "Oh, 10, 12, however many God sends me." I had the same reaction to that as he had when I said "I'm not marrying someone who hasn't saved himself for me." I thought, *Man, this guy is crazy.* But later on when I reflected on it, I realized this guy values family. He likes kids. Maybe I'd better rethink trying to blow him off. That was the beginning of the turning point.

The other thing that I found very interesting about these conversations was the way he helped me to reconsider some of my anti-Catholic views. I wasn't mean-spiritedly anti-Catholic; I had just mis-learned a lot of things while growing up. I went to Catholic schools for 12 years and I received the sacraments, so I was technically Catholic. But I wasn't really brought up Catholic. My parents didn't teach us anything about Catholicism. In fact, we stopped attending Mass when I was in sixth grade. And so I was technically a Catholic, but I was a functional Protestant. When our mutual friend told Chris that I was a Catholic, he said it in good faith because he didn't know how far gone I was. Had he known, I doubt he would have introduced me to Chris. So I'm glad he didn't know.

Anyway, I asked Chris one day, "What do you view as more important, your relationship with God or your relationship with the Church?" And he gave me an answer that I remember to this day, because it pulled me up so short. He said, "I view my relationship with God as being one and the same as my relationship with the Church." I had never heard a Catholic say that. I had never met a Catholic, other than our mutual friends who introduced us, who knew their faith at all. I had never known a Catholic who actually tried to live what they professed to believe. And I had never met a Catholic who knew anything about the Bible. I certainly had never met a Catholic who went to Mass every day. Here was this clearly intelligent, well-spoken guy who believed in God and the Church. He really had that personal relationship with Jesus Christ that Protestants talk about. So that put me on the road back to the sacraments; and coupled with the fact that he appeared to like children, made me think twice about trying to blow him off. That's when things took off between us, and I agreed to a first date, which was in January of 1994.

Chris: I'm from Seattle originally, and went out there at Christmas time. I'd brought a fresh salmon back to Michigan, so I invited her over to have salmon. Then we planned to meet up with her parents to watch a college basketball game that her brother was in town coaching.

Micki: He'd been asking me repeatedly to go out. Finally, I said, I will go out with you on one condition: we're going to a basketball game and you're going to meet my folks. You can make me dinner beforehand, but we are going to this ball game, and we are going with my parents, and that's just the way it is. I guess he was glad I agreed to go out with him at all, so he was willing to agree to anything. I insisted that he meet my parents, because I knew if he could get past my father, then he was worth taking seriously. Being the youngest kid in my family, and being the youngest girl, I think my dad kind of feared me finding 'that someone special.' So when I told him I had a young man I wanted him to meet, my mild-mannered, very calm and gentle father went ballistic. He hit the roof, and I was in tears at the end of the conversation. I figured if Chris could survive my dad, then I would consider going out with him a second time.

Chris: So I made salmon at my place, and then we went from there to the ball game. And I met her father and he was a...

Micki: He was a cream puff.

Chris: Yeah, I don't know, maybe it was just the way I looked or something but, for whatever reason, he didn't light into me. And we hit it off and we enjoyed talking to each other through the ball game.

Micki: On the way back to his place to get my car, Chris asked, "Would you like me to drive down to your parents' place tomorrow and pick you up and take you to Mass?" I said, "Sure."

I wasn't quite sure what my dad had thought of Chris, because my dad is kind of like me: he'll talk to pretty much anybody, even if he dislikes them. I was trying to figure out how to explain to my dad that this guy was going to pick me up and take me to Mass. The next morning, I'm still trying to figure out how to break it to my dad that Chris is coming to pick me up. I never did figure out how to do that. I was all dressed up and my dad said, "Why are you all dressed up?" I said, "I'm going to go to Church this morning." He was sitting there in his pajamas when Chris drove up. My parents live up on a hill and there's this long driveway. Dad looked out the window and asked, "Who's that driving up the driveway?" I took a deep breath and told him, "That's Chris. He's coming to take me to Mass." My dad pounded his fist on the table. *Oh, here it comes*, I thought. But he said, "Why didn't you tell me he was coming? I would have invited him to breakfast!" At that point, I realized that my dad likes this guy. So, I decided I was going to take Chris seriously. A few months later, however, he tried to break up with me.

Chris: The thing was, in April I learned I'd been accepted to graduate school in Los Angeles, and would be starting that coming fall or winter. I had tried doing the long distance relationship thing before, and it'd been a disaster.

Since Micki and I had only been seeing each other for a few months, I thought it would be best to nip this in the bud before it became a long and drawn out thing. I should say that we were kind of long distance already; she was a few hundred miles away, but we could get together on weekends. If I was in California, getting together would be a major production. So on April 15, I told her I thought it would be best if we kind of broke this off. Basically, she refused to hang up the phone first.

Micki: I argued with him for an hour and a half, and then I refused to hang up. I figured Chris was being stupid and unilateral, and that he just needed to talk a little more to realize he was being stupid and unilateral. Then he asked me to hang up. I wasn't going to do it, because that was also stupid and unilateral. So that's kind of the way it went.

Chris: By the end of the conversation, I reconsidered. Things went fine for the rest of that year. Once I actually got out to Los Angeles, in January, I started seriously questioning whether staying together was a good idea. But as I thought more about it, just the idea of her not being in my life, there was this great big gaping hole. I knew at that point that it was inevitable that we were going to get married.

Micki: I think what happened was we got into this big argument and I said something flip and dumb. "Fine, why don't we just give each other up for Lent?" Chris said, "That's a great idea." I didn't really mean it. He said, "I do."

So we gave each other up for Lent and we didn't talk for – it was only a couple of days. I called one of my friends and bawled my head off. While I was talking to him, Chris called back. So we gave each other up for Lent for two days.

Chris: Then I proposed on Palm Sunday and we were married the middle of September, 1995.

Now, thinking of regrets or things I would have done differently in our courtship, in our engaged period, there are a couple things.

First, I was almost too well versed in the writings of Blessed John Paul II, what is now called The Theology of the Body. I don't think it was called that then, but I had read almost all of it. What that had given me was almost impossibly high ideals and aspirations about marriage. I saw marriage as a kind of participation in the inner life of the Trinity, which is all true. These are good things to know. But I had gone too far in this theoretically, and hadn't thought enough about the practicalities of it. That's what led me to want to have as many kids as possible, which I see now was a very unrealistic attitude.

Another mistake was that I didn't want to learn Natural Family Planning (NFP) before we were married. I saw NFP as a cop-out for people who didn't want to go all the way in giving of themselves. In my mind, there would never be a good enough reason to postpone pregnancy, to keep me from participating in God's creative power, in the inner life of the Trinity. When I'm thinking of sex and marriage and procreation, why would I ever want to hold back from that? I came to seriously regret that attitude. What I quickly learned is that everyone ought to learn NFP before they're married. Even if you don't want to postpone the first pregnancy, NFP is an important tool that everyone should have available. You may think now that you'll never need it, but you almost certainly will run into different circumstances later. It's a tool you'll really wish you had. NFP is *much* easier to learn before your first pregnancy.

Micki: At that time, I knew enough about my cycle to know that I was going to be in my fertile period on our honeymoon; so I had suggested that we learn NFP during our engagement.

Chris: We did end up having a honeymoon baby, and we have no regrets about that.

There are aspects about marriage that are wonderful and blissful and, in some respects, perfect. But this is the thing: you don't know ahead of time what those are going to be. When we were engaged, I knew intellectually that there would be difficulties and conflicts, but I figured that we'd be having sex all the time, so that would make up for the difficulties and help us get through. That turned out to be laughably wrong.

Micki: Marriage has taught me how to die to myself for the good of another, out of love for another. That's something you cannot learn if your life is always easy. I'm grateful that God has allowed me the crosses, because they are making me into the person, I hope, that He wants me to be. God has Chris and me together because we're supposed to help each other get to heaven. But by loving and serving God, our spouses, and our children, we will find true happiness and we will help ourselves, our spouses and our children to get to heaven. And that's what it's all about anyway.

*Chris and Micki's last name has been changed for personal reasons.

Chris holds a PhD in political science and has his own public opinion research consulting practice. Micki is a former attorney and is currently a homeschooling mother. Their four children range in age from fifteen years to eighteen months. They live on a farm in rural mid-Michigan where they raise dairy goats, chickens, ducks, geese, turkeys and sheep.

Chris and Micki and family

James and Pati Mikulasik

Married October 11, 2002

It's God's Will That We Get Married

James and Pati 2001

Pati: The first time I saw James was in October of 1989. I was going up to a cabin with a girlfriend of mine, and we thought that we had it to ourselves for the weekend. It was her parents' cabin, and her brother had the same idea, and he invited James up for the weekend to bow hunt. My friend and I were just settling in and making a nice dinner for ourselves when, all of a sudden, there were two men dressed in hunting garb at the door. Before that, I had heard of this big Canadian logger coming to work on NET (National Evangelization Team) staff. All I remember was that he had a very big smile. He looked very country-ish.

James: Especially in my camouflage.

Pati: I had decided at that time in my life that I wasn't going to date. I was kind of new in my faith. I had always been Catholic, but I was newly evangelized. I made the decision year after year not to date until 1993. When I felt that I was open to dating, that's when James asked me out.

James: I'm originally from British Columbia, Canada. From 1988 to 1989, I volunteered for NET Ministries down in St. Paul, Minnesota. Then I was asked to be on the volunteer staff for NET, so I came back down to the States the next year. I was one of 20 people on staff.

Pati was part of this other group called St. Paul's Outreach, which is a Catholic organization that reaches out to college students. There were times that we had formation together, and that's where we started to get to know each other with mutual Catholic friends. I think I was crazy about her from the first time I saw her. One of the things that was neat is that we both really liked dancing. We always had a lot of fun too.

It has been the policy for those volunteering with NET not to date the entire year while you're on the road, and then they recommend waiting at least six months afterwards, and I was fine with that. I wasn't against dating, but I was enjoying being single in a really beautiful environment with all these other single people. We were just doing ministry together and it was awesome. It wasn't like it was a strategic thing as far as not dating, but it just wasn't the time.

It was a couple of years until I thought that it might be nice to start dating. That's when I found out through mutual friends that Pati wasn't available for dating, so I started dating some great Catholic girls, but still had my heart set on Pati. That's how it began. Then, again through mutual friends, I heard that Pati was open to dating, so that's when I asked her out.

We went out three times and each time it was nice. I enjoyed myself and it was very, very good. I thought it was going great. I also thought that I really was falling for her, and I told her that. Actually, I told her that I thought it's God's will that we get married, that we be together. And she just laughed.

Pati: By the third date, I had decided that James was definitely not the kind of man I would ever want to marry. So I thought I would have to nip this in the bud before I made things any worse. I told him that I didn't want to go out with him anymore, that he was a great guy, but he just wasn't what I had in mind. That's when he said, with a big smile, "No, no, no, it's God's will that we be together," and I just laughed and said, "If it's God's will, He's going to tell me too. He's not just going to tell you." So that was it. In '93, we stopped dating.

To sum it up, I guess James seemed too much of a "hick" for me. I saw myself with someone more refined and cultured. I just couldn't get past that in him. I think I was very idealistic and didn't know myself very well either.

At this point I met a group of religious sisters that I really liked. I didn't really want to join the religious life, so it was more of a decision of despair, I think. I was 28 years old and I had dated these great guys, and none of them did anything for me. I felt like I couldn't stand the idea of being single all my life, as that would be a fate worse than death. So I thought that I'd rather be a sister, even though that sounded horrible to me.

I joined the sisters really just thinking, *Well, I think I can do this.* I really want to get to heaven, and this will be a way that I'm pretty much sure that I'll get to heaven. So that's really why I chose religious life. I was very unhappy for six and a half years. But I was very obedient and good at doing what I was asked to do. It was in '94 that I entered, the same year James left NET USA and decided to bring NET to Canada.

James: I started up NET Canada in July. It was a very busy time in my life, just getting that all rolling. I didn't have a lot of time to date, although there were a lot of beautiful single people, and I was still feeling called to marriage. I talked to my spiritual director and he agreed, yes, marriage was probably the vocation for me. I dated some beautiful Catholic girls. I knew I wanted to marry a Catholic girl, but I always had Pati in the back of my mind.

A friend of ours, Meg, called me out of the blue in June of 2001, and she said, "Oh, James, how are you doing?" I said, "Hi Meg, I haven't talked to you in ten years. How are you?" She said, "Good." I said, "Who are you trying to set me up with, Meg?" She said, "Do you know that Pati Donohue is out of the convent?" I said, "I had no idea. Do you know I've already been down that road with Pati?" She said, "Yes, but I think you should talk to her." So she gave me Pati's number and I gave her a call.

Pati: Meg told me after she had already called James. We went out for coffee and she said "What are you looking for in a man?" I was looking for somebody who was a real thinker, and someone who loved Pope John Paul II and who was really alive in his faith – I can't remember what other qualities I had listed off to her.

She said, "You know, I think James Mikulasik really fits that," and I just laughed. I said, "Not at all." She said, "You never gave him a chance."

I said, "I broke his heart and I really don't see any hope there; I'm not interested."

She said, "Well, I already called him and I gave him your number."

So I was pretty mad at her for that, but I thought, *Well, I'm a big girl and he's big boy and we'll deal with it.* If he gives me a call, I'll talk to him.

He gave me a call sometime in mid-June. He was coming down to visit NET USA in July, so he asked if he could see me when he was in town.

As soon as I heard his voice, it was like talking to an old friend. I was happy to see him again, even though I really didn't have any intention of it going anywhere.

James: I think that when I was starting to re-date Pati (dating Pati Part II), it was just like putting it in the Lord's hand and saying, *Lord, here is this relationship. I still have feelings for Pati, I'm just going to abandon it to You and whatever You want, it's Your will, Your will be done.* I think that was a key thing.

One really cool thing that happened during our first date down there in Minnesota was this: as we were going for a walk outside of St. Paul, there was a beautiful full moon. I really felt like Our Lady's hand was on us, like Our Lady was just watching over us, and taking care of us during that time. It was the most beautiful full moon I had ever seen.

Pati: It's funny because I walked out of the restaurant and I also saw the full moon over the river. I thought, *Oh no, that looks like a sign.*

Taking it back to the beginning of the night, I had purposely dressed quite casually, because I didn't want to get anything started. As soon as I opened the door, there was a look in his eyes and I knew that nothing had changed as far as he was concerned. He was still in love with me. What surprised me was that I didn't mind, even though I had been kind of preparing myself, *Keep it down, you don't want to lead him on; you don't want to hurt him again.* I kind of liked the look in his eye and that surprised me, the first little surprise.

Our date was very enjoyable. We have so many mutual friends and so many mutual memories, and it was just a really nice time to catch up. But a couple times during the meal, I caught that same look in his eye, and I was just bewildered that it didn't bother me. I think that's as far as it went for me, though. I had taken off the veil in December, and this was only July. So I still felt like my ears were exposed. I was really adjusting to the fact that I wasn't a sister anymore. In fact, when he came down for the weekend, I told him, "We can go out Friday night, but after that, I don't know. That might be it. I might not be able to handle any more than that." After Friday night, he said, "Can I see you tomorrow?" I said, "Well, call me in the morning; I'll see how I feel." I wasn't sure how much I could take of this. Then we ended up going out that Saturday night. He called me on Sunday and I said "No, I couldn't handle Sunday." Then he called me Monday and I said, "Yes, we could go out on Monday." But I just wanted to go to a park or something simple.

That Monday night when we were leaving the park, James was going to drive me back to my parents' house, where I was living, and he basically confessed his love for me. I didn't know how to respond, so I didn't say anything. A few moments of silence went by, and he said, "You have to talk to me, Pati. You need to tell me what you're thinking. Whatever it is, just tell me what you're thinking."

I said, "Well, I think you have virtue up the wazoo, but I'm not attracted to you. I don't see this going anywhere. I really don't want to break your heart again, and that's all I can foresee."

He said, "My heart is my responsibility. And I'm willing to take that risk."

Then he said, "I would just really like to see you again."

There was something about that, well, it's true, his heart *is* his responsibility. If my only reason for not seeing him again is because I don't want to hurt him, he was saying, "Let me make that decision." So I said, "Okay, I'll let you see me again." When he dropped me off in the driveway, his last words were, "How often can I call you?" I said, "I don't know." He said, "Well, can I call you every day?" I said, "Well, you can call me every day, and if it gets to be too much, I'll let you know." Then he said, "Can I write you letters? Can I send you flowers?" I said, "Yeah, I guess you could do that."

What was funny is that about two weeks before, this other man from Canada had come down, kind of a blind date, and we had gone out about three or four times. The last night he was leaving, he dropped me off in the same place in my parent's driveway, and I said to him, "Well, where do we go from here? Are we going to call? Are we going to write or..." He said, "Well, you have my number." I thought, *I do not have your number anymore. The first thing I'm going to do is throw it away.* This guy had everything I was looking for. He was a philosophy professor. He spoke several languages fluently. He could salsa dance like nothing, and he was very suave. Yet those were his final words.

Then James, who was not at all what I was looking for, as far as all those kinds of qualities, his last words to me in the exact same spot were, "How often can I call you?" That really hit home for me. It was the first wake up call that I was looking for the wrong things in men.

James: During that weekend, she said, "Well, I'm just not attracted to you." I said, "Well, let's just take it in baby steps here. Compared to the beginning of the weekend, do you like me more or do you like me less?" She said, "Well, a little bit more, yeah." I said, "Well, when you start liking me less, you let me know. Let's just take it in stride here."

Pati: James said, "Why don't we just keep going out until you find that you're liking me less?" I couldn't argue with that. So I thought, *Okay, I can do that.*

Over the next three or four months of our dating, I regularly tried to end it and would say, "You know what, James? All I see is that I'm just going to break your heart again. I can just feel it. It's going to end in nothing and you're going to be heartbroken," and he would come up with something again that would be very beautiful and very manly. I would say "Okay" again, and he would give me whatever it was to keep going.

I attribute a lot of my falling in love with James to his perseverance, which I admired.

I admired his courage. I admired his humility in the way

that he dealt with me. I thought any normal man would've walked away a million times. What is it about this guy that he just won't give up? I was convinced that he really did love me and that was not a question for me at all. I really enjoyed spending time with him. I just didn't know if I could love him back.

In October, I decided to come up to live in Canada so we would not be dating long distance. My job was very easy to leave. Then I went back home to Minnesota for Christmas. While I was home at Christmas time, I was looking through some photos that I had taken of us. I was looking at a picture of James and I was looking at his eyes. I was really struck by the kindness in his eyes. I was really struck by, *This man loves me.* I realized then that I really loved him too, that I loved who he was, I loved how he loved me, and I loved how I was when I was with him. So at that moment, it was like, *Oh wow.* That's what happened.

James: When she told me, my reaction was, "Okay, is this for real?" I was a little doubtful, I think. But I was absolutely excited and happy. I said, "Okay. All the way along you've been saying how you're not attracted to me and now, all of a sudden, you are? And that's great and I'm glad." But I just wanted to make sure it was for real. I said, "Let's just keep going, and this is awesome, this is beautiful that we're growing in love for one another. Let's just see where God leads this."

Pati: Up until this time, he had pretty much said to me, "You say the word and we're married tomorrow." Then once I did say "Okay, yeah, I'm ready to get married tomorrow," he said, "Whoa, whoa, whoa, let's take some time, to be sure we're doing the right thing." I think there was something of the hunt that was over, and there was a bit of the reality of what was actually happening.

James: One of the things all the way along, you always have these preconceived notions of how you want it to be when you're going to get married. I have a strong sense of providing and protecting as a man. At that time, it was probably the worst time of financial stress that I had been in in a long time. It kind of rocked my world as far as trust in the Lord and as far as our relationship and going ahead with the marriage. I couldn't even afford to buy her a ring.

Pati: That was huge for him and I think he was having a hard time telling me that. From my point of view, all of a sudden, the brakes are put on, and I couldn't figure out why for quite a while. I really had to convince him that that didn't matter to me. I was good at being poor. I had been poor all my life so I didn't care if he had money. I didn't even care if he had debt. I didn't care if I had a ring. It wasn't about that. Anyway, we got engaged in May.

James: Actually, I told Pati I wanted us to have some time together. It was such a busy time of our life. We were preparing for World Youth Day in Canada. Pati was helping us in that, in our ministry in NET. It was a really busy time. So I said, "Let's take a retreat and just take some time." We went on a seven-day silent Ignatian retreat; and it was very good.

Pati: I really felt clear. This was it. He was the one.

James: I did too. I just wanted to hear it from the Lord. It was a very, very blessed retreat. There were a lot of things that happened on the retreat that really spoke to me. It was like, "Yeah, this is the girl that you were made for. She's a beautiful person." She's going to be a beautiful wife and a beautiful mother, and it was confirmed by God that this is the gal for me.

Pati: It was the right decision.

James: I wanted to propose in a place that was going to be there forever, not bulldozed over by developers. We're both Irish, so I proposed to her May 24th, 2002 in St. Patrick's Basilica in Ottawa.

Pati: We got married in St. Paul, Minnesota at St. Paul's Cathedral on October 11th, 2002.

James: It was Thanksgiving Day in Canada.

One of the things I wanted to mention was, at least for me, I had a really beautiful single life. I was 38 when Pati and I started dating again and before that, I was saying, "I feel called to marriage, but here is my vocation. You've got to provide me with the one you want me to marry." We got married when I was 39 and Pati was 36. So it was kind of like God saying, "Okay. I've taken care of you." I think that was a really beautiful confirmation that the Lord is looking out for us.

James and Pati and their two sons live near Ottawa, Ontario. James is a developer (of many things) and the founder of NET Ministries of Canada. Pati stays home "developing" their boys ages 7 and 5.

The Mikulasik Family

Robert and Sarah Reinhard

Married November 29, 2003

Atheist Meets Catholic Prince Charming

Robert and Sarah 2002

Sarah: Once upon a time...isn't that how every romance begins? I never imagined that I would meet Prince Charming for real.

As a little girl, I dreamed of being a princess. My name, after all, means "princess" in Hebrew. I was a tomboy, though, and my version of princesshood involved climbing trees and exploring outdoors. My nose was in a book as often as I could get it there, except, of course, when I was off seeking adventure.

I met my Prince Charming after my illusions of royalty were long gone. By the time I was working at the country's largest John Deere dealership after college, I was cynical and rather atheist. God had proven that He didn't exist as far as I was concerned.

Though I had been raised Christian – mostly Methodist, with some non-denominational charismatic varieties thrown in – I was convinced that reason and logic disproved the supernatural.

Robert: I had been raised Catholic, attended Catholic schools from first grade to graduation, and so I never knew any different. It was an irrevocable part of my life.

Sarah: We had many long conversations over the back parts counter at the dealership, when he looked at me and was actually interested in what I had to say (instead of where listening could lead).

I found out about his faith life after I had been on a date and bared parts of myself no one else had really cared to hear about; I found out quite by accident. We were on the phone, planning a hiking date for a Sunday, when he said, in his typically no-nonsense way, that he couldn't get to my place before 10, because he went to 8:30 Mass.

This is the man who couldn't talk before about 10, getting up to go to church? Just what was so special about Mass that he would want to go? Well, I didn't care enough then to pursue it beyond a little smile at the fact. But as we continued to date, six months, then a year, I did get curious. What was so special about Mass? How could it be better than time spent with me?

Robert: I had only just started attending Mass again. I had gone two or three years without it and had been far from regular for the ten years prior to that.

Sarah: His mother was very devout and very excited about her faith. *Yeah,* I thought, *she's just that way. Some people like to sew, she likes to be Catholic. It's her thing. Big deal.*

I had decided to go and see what Mass was all about. The colorful stories about Father Pat enticed me and, I reasoned, they have a book that tells you what to do – they must be pretty organized in the Catholic Church, and I value organization a great deal. That first Mass, and for about the next year, Bob held my hand and sat with me and encouraged me. He didn't ever say anything about me joining the Church. He didn't ever express that he did or did not prefer that his future wife be Catholic. He didn't have to.

I used to justify that, rationally and logically, God was a silly notion that was both irrational and illogical. *Come on!* I would cry in my mind, this makes no sense and besides, none of these defenders of God's use rational or logical arguments.

In my upbringing, I saw the stalwart Methodists and the charismatic Baptists. I spent a good part of my before-bed prayer time wondering if I should be speaking in tongues, as the Evangelical non-denominationals insisted we should. It didn't take long for me to wonder why it was so wonderful to be saved...and saved...and saved. I was saved at least three times, telling Jesus that He was welcome in my heart. But what if being five made that not count? My mother recounted a story to me where, when I was three, I had asked Jesus into my heart. But at twelve, knowing that I certainly hadn't held up my end of the "good Christian" bargain, I asked Him again. Because, you know, you can never be too saved, can you? And if you can be saved more than once, how do you know which one counts for good?

Robert: I, for my part, kept silent. I had my own struggle with the Catholic faith. As well, my older brother and I were the main providers for our family for ten years before I met Sarah.

As Sarah wondered about the value of the Catholic Church, I found myself coming home. I sat with her at Mass and felt the comfort of the routine and the ritual. I woke up early on Sunday mornings because I desired that peace.

My life had been a maelstrom as my parents struggled, but the Church remained unwavering, and I found I needed that. In the years directly following my coming home to the Church, my family would weather some major storms, including my parents' divorce and annulment and the death of my sister's baby.

Sarah: By the time I had decided to set foot in a Catholic church, there was a part of me that recognized that the relationship we were building was worth something as silly (I thought then) as marriage. So many people divorced, so many families torn apart: wasn't your family comprised of more than just the many step-families you might have accumulated?

After I met Bob and the thought of marrying him occurred to me, I was alarmed. Was I not a contemporary thinker, freed of such antiquated ideas as marriage? Hadn't I experienced divorce twice in my own family, and hadn't I seen how much havoc it wreaked, how much pain it caused, how much hurt it sowed?

I had been attending Mass for a few months when our priest gave a homily on Mothers Day about Mary, our Mother. He talked about how we all have a mother who is unconditional, who is waiting for us, who understands our trials and tribulations. His words spoke to my soul, and for the first time, my hard heart melted. Unprepared for this, I began crying, and then sobbing. I had to leave the sanctuary. I perched on the steps to the choir loft in the vestibule, and after the recessional at the end of Mass, Father asked me if I was okay. I could only nod. What was this Church?

It was not unusual for the Mass to make me cry, which always embarrassed me. I learned to take tissues, but it always troubled me that I cried. Was there something wrong with me? I reasoned that it must be the beauty of the ritual. Having read quite a bit of Joseph Campbell, I had already justified all of the wonderful things about the Catholic Church in light of ritual and man's need for mythology. I laugh now when I think of how I was still trying to be rational and logical using the world's reasoning.

Robert: I saw it all as out of my hands. I believed that it was up to the Holy Spirit. I never tried to persuade Sarah or discuss her conversion process. I listened, but I continued to be impartial.

Sarah: That was, perhaps, the most convincing thing he could have done. I got just the support and encouragement from him that I needed.

That Lent, before Easter 2001, Father talked about the sacrifices we should make. "Lent shouldn't just be about giving up chocolate," he said. "It should be about giving up a bad habit and becoming permanently better." What a concept! I decided that my Lenten "project" would be forgiving my mother and mending my relationship with her. It took me all forty days, but I composed a letter to her, explaining that I was wrong to have turned my back on her, and that if she would forgive me for my hard heart, I would like to have a relationship with her. The ensuing scenes only emphasized to me that I was doing the right thing. The calm I felt in my heart reassured me. My Mother Mary was with me, holding me, encouraging me.

Through my journey to the Catholic Church, Bob was beside me, gently holding my hand, guiding me and supporting me. He never said much, though I'm sure he must have prayed a great deal. I never doubted that what he offered me was love unlike any I had known, love that reflected the Love he knew from his Catholic past.

We dated for five years, and during that time I became Catholic and became more comfortable as a Catholic. Though there was never a doubt that we would marry, and marry Catholic, there was never a hurry about it. It wasn't until the summer of 2003, when I made two unexpected trips across the country for a family visit and a funeral, that Bob felt inspired to propose. We were married that fall, in the Catholic Church where we had dated and where, in the years since, our children have been baptized.

The Reinhard Family live in Ohio. Robert is an electrical engineer and Sarah is a "Catholic convert/wife/mom/reader/writer," who enjoys the idiosyncrasies of life on a farm with critters and kids. She writes online at www.snoringscholar.com. and is the author of "Welcome Baby Jesus: Advent & Christmas Reflections for Families."

The Reinhard Family

Tom and Patty Strunck

Married May 23, 1987

Is God Calling You?

Tom and Patty 1986

Patty: I was my father's 30th birthday present, although I did arrive four days earlier than his actual birthday. It was my claim to fame in our family. Because I was the middle of five children and the middle girl, I needed something to set me apart from the rest.

When my younger brother turned five, my mom began to take classes at a local college to earn a nursing degree. I was fascinated by her stethoscope. Our next door neighbor's daughter watched over us when we got home from school, and we went to day care in the summer. Mom was busy with her studies and later with her job at the hospital; Dad traveled frequently for his work. As we grew older, we no longer needed the babysitting. We became "latch-key" kids before that phrase entered popular jargon.

In high school, the party was at our house, at least until Mom got home from work.

We did not practice religion so I had no saintly role models. The females I admired were found on the television set: Kate Jackson on "Charlie's Angels" was one of my favorites. I was a sponge for what the culture thought was important. Legalized abortion, the Equal Rights Amendment, and no-fault divorce were just some of the issues I believed were necessary for the advancement of women. Sadly, my family experienced one of those issues first-hand when my parents divorced after 25 years of marriage. Although I was a senior in high school, their broken relationship left a scar.

Tom: My relationship with Patty McNair started years before I ever knew who she was. While young, I was shy with girls and easily fell into schoolboy crushes that never amounted to anything. During one teenage crush, I decided to do something constructive: I prayed a Rosary for the girl every day. It took a couple of months to realize that relationship was going the same way as all the others – nowhere – so I was inspired to change the intention of the Rosary to "my future wife and children."

Patty: In my junior year of high school, I was "in love," a relationship that lasted three years. He was a year older, and it felt so good that this cute guy liked me. I followed him to college. We broke up during my freshman year because we were too young and immature.

Immediately after that break-up, my second long-term relationship began. I enjoyed the security of having a boyfriend and we were a couple through my remaining three years of college. We broke up during my first year of law school. After that, my life was full with studying and partying with my law school friends, so the need for a boyfriend, though still present, was not as strong.

During my third year of law school, my father developed a cough which was diagnosed as pneumonia; however, that diagnosis was altered to lung cancer upon the discovery of a tumor in his left lung. Dad decided he would not have surgery or chemotherapy but would use radiation to shrink any tumors. That decision would hasten his death.

Tom: I prayed a Rosary for my future family nearly every night through my last years of high school. In college, my praying grew irregular, but one common intention was "my future wife and children." After graduating in 1984, I attended law school, where I met Patty. She was a year ahead of me and hung out with a popular and partying crowd. Although she was undeniably cute, I found her somewhat obnoxious. Most especially, I did not like the way she laughed.

One fall day in 1985, while descending the escalator outside the school library, I noticed Patty with a group of her friends. Something about her particularly struck me. I walked past the group and briefly pondered whether to ask her on a date. As I opened the door to exit the building, I was briefly overcome by an unusually intense thought, as if someone was speaking to me, but not audibly. The voice said, "*You are going to marry her.*" With the door half open, I froze, at least until Patty's obnoxious laugh came floating down the hall. "*Not only am I not going to marry her,*" I said to myself, "*I will never go out with her.*" I continued outside, shaking my head.

In January 1986, I was attracted to a flirtatious law school classmate. She and Patty were friends. I invited my classmate to an upcoming dance, but she already had a date. She suggested I take Patty instead. So Patty and I went to the dance together, double-dating with my classmate and her boyfriend. The dance turned out to be a lot of fun. Patty was outgoing and easy to talk to.

Patty: Tom was cute and I needed a date. We had a nice time together. Initially, I thought that Tom was not my type; he was a little awkward and stiff. But there was something about him that was different from other men I had known. He treated me with respect. We kept dating each other through my last semester of law school.

Tom: Before Patty, I had never dated the same girl more than three consecutive times. With Patty, spending time together was natural and I never noticed we were on our fourth, fifth or sixth date. I enjoyed doing anything or nothing at all with her. After a couple of weeks, she told me that her father had been diagnosed with lung cancer and refused chemotherapy. Over time, his declining health would serve as the glue for our increasingly shaky relationship.

Patty: Dating Tom and Dad's cancer intensified at roughly the same time. The more ill Dad became, the more I needed Tom. This was especially true when my car broke down, because Dad had always taken care of my automotive needs. When he was unable to do this, Tom became my chauffeur. We spent lots of time together. He came from a devout Catholic family and was able to answer questions I had concerning suffering, life, death, and God. Still, Tom was not someone I would consider marrying. I was 24, emotionally immature, and not even thinking of marriage.

Tom: Although Patty was not thinking about marriage, over several months of dating, the thought had crossed my mind. Even so, Patty and I were not deeply compatible. She had no religion while I was undergoing a somewhat rocky renaissance in my spiritual life. We frequently clashed over politics and morality and I thought these disagreements would be unhealthy for our future children.

Patty: As Dad's cancer progressed, Tom invited me to attend Easter Mass at Holy Spirit Catholic Church, which was two blocks from my house. I found it deeply moving, so much so, that I continued to attend every Sunday. I enjoyed Mass, but with my dad in such poor health, I was very confused. Tom was the best man I had ever dated, as he kiddingly reminded me at the time, but I wanted something more to fill the growing hole in my heart.

Tom: Going to Mass together was a comforting experience, especially given her father's declining health. But it could not make up for our differences. Several weeks before her graduation from law school she suggested we see other people. I was disappointed because I really liked her, but mostly, my pride was offended. I told her to make a choice: see me alone or never see me again. If it hadn't been for her broken-down car and continuing need for rides, our relationship would have ended then.

After her father entered the final month of his life, things changed dramatically. Patty needed stability. She started asking profound questions about God and what happens after death. My improved understanding of Catholic theology offered a frame of reference and sense of trust that helped us cope with her dad's illness. Although I had questions about our relationship in the long term, I decided it would be cowardly and unchristian to abandon her.

Patty: When Dad entered the hospital for the last week of his life, Tom was a rock for me. Out of fear or discomfort, my sisters' boyfriends stayed away from my father. Tom's ability to be at the hospital bed, praying the Rosary as life was leaving Dad's body, showed me that he was a keeper.

Tom: While her father was in the hospital, Patty spent nearly every day with him. She cared for him, read scripture and studied for the bar exam for hours in his room. The closer he got to death, the closer Patty and I grew together. She called me anytime there were changes and the family thought he might not survive. I was most honored to be present the night he died. I got down on my knees and prayed a Rosary about two hours before his final breath. Her step-mother let me give him a brown scapular. At one point, Patty asked, "Where's the priest?" What could I tell her? Her father was not Catholic. She was expressing the universal human need for a symbol of something more than an empty hole after this life. He died on June 3, 1986, about a half hour after my birthday, on June 2nd, had ended.

After her father's death, Patty transferred a lot of affection to me, as if I was replacing her dad. I was simultaneously relieved and a little uncomfortable. It was a very intense time and I sensed that something profound was taking place. So did my mom and dad. One morning, speaking of my relationship with Patty, my dad made a prophetic observation. He told me: "Loving is very close to love." In my case, loving (sacrificing oneself for another) would be followed closely by love (giving oneself away to another).

Watching Patty with her dying dad was deeply impressive. I saw genuine faithfulness, which I appreciate now as her finest personal quality. Here was someone who would stick it out in bad times as well as good. This experience was an epiphany; not only were Patty and I close as friends, but she had the substance I longed for in a wife and mother of my children.

Patty: The comfort I found during Mass helped to ease the anguish I felt over Dad's death. The more frequently I attended Mass, the more I longed to receive Our Lord in the Blessed Sacrament. Six weeks after Dad died, Tom proposed. I believed it was a sympathy proposal, but I accepted.

Tom: On July 13, 1986, six weeks after her father died, I proposed. I didn't know this at the time, but it was the anniversary of her parents' own marriage. Our decision to marry, however, was emotional; we were still wrapped up in all that had happened. Although we felt strongly for each other, our fundamental moral differences were not ideal ingredients for parenting. She had accepted raising our children Catholic, but how could her vocal contradictory values not undermine their faith? Taking time to reconsider is one of the purposes of an engagement, so for a time I pondered whether to withdraw.

Patty: After Tom proposed, I came to realize the importance of our family embracing one faith. I welcomed the opportunity to be accepted into the Church. For the next ten months, I did some heavy soul-searching. Tom's catholicity was a vital part of who he was. I longed for that connection to God, but I had to understand Church teaching on social issues, particularly those related to women, in order to take the next step of the RCIA (Rite of Christian Initiation for Adults) process. Tom gave me the space to do this. If he had made my conversion mandatory to our marriage, I wouldn't have done either.

Tom: From the moment we first agreed to marry, we avoided discussing the subjects of religion, politics and morality. Initially, I feared the lack of discussion meant trouble for the marriage; but it turned out to be wise. Patty needed space. After she started RCIA, we began to discuss delicate matters again. Her conversion was intense. It affected the way she analyzed issues. Ironically, Catholic teaching fit her like a glove. She became, and remains, more profoundly and practically Catholic than I am. It would have been impossible had I not given her the room she needed to think.

Patty: The priest who prepared us for marriage was the same priest I met to get information on RCIA. We enjoyed our appointments with him. He was newly ordained and we were one of the first couples he prepared. Tom and I did exceptionally well on the diocesan compatibility test, except for the finance section. We discussed everything, including family planning and family size. Tom is one of six and I am one of five. We both wanted a large family. We agreed to use Natural Family Planning when it was time to space our children.

Tom: For years I had wondered whether God would answer my high school prayers. During our engagement, it became clear those prayers were the most vibrant and successful of my life. Hoping to build on that success, I started attending daily Mass and regularly going to Confession. I thought it critical to involve God as much as possible in our upcoming marriage. But there was one more hurdle to cross before I was ready to give myself away to Patty completely. I have a miserable tendency to sometimes over-analyze and regret my decisions. I believe God found an unforgettable way to use my personal weakness to help protect against my ever questioning the decision to marry.

What happened next is one of the most remarkable experiences of my life.

While frequenting the sacraments, I developed a serious interest in theology. Theology of the Body was not taught in marriage preparation classes yet, so instead of seeing marriage as a holy vocation filled with theological significance, I began to confuse my newfound passion with a potential vocation to the priesthood.

It didn't help that, only months before the wedding, I heard two homilies the same week about the obligation to respond to religious vocations. One of the priests even said that ignoring a religious vocation early in life could lead to dissatisfaction later in life. Unsure whether I had mistakenly rejected a vocation to the priesthood as a younger man, I grew increasingly anxious.

One day after daily Mass, and approximately eight weeks before the wedding, I begged God for a sign. It was March 1987, and I was in St. John's Catholic Church, where my family had been going to Mass for years. Like most Catholic churches, it had a pamphlet rack at its entrance. I long remembered a pamphlet there entitled "Is God Calling You?" that encouraged religious vocations. When I was eleven years old, I had promised God while in St. John's that I would one day be a priest if He would grant me a favor. (My family had recently moved and I was begging God for friends.) During adolescence, I avoided looking at that pamphlet because it reminded me of that promise.

Going to Mass that March morning, "Is God Calling You?" was located in the upper left-hand corner of the rack. On that day, that tiny pamphlet appeared to be the size of a highway billboard. While praying the rosary after Mass, I vowed to God that if the same pamphlet was there the following day, I would call off the wedding and consider the priesthood. But before leaving church, I checked to see how many "Is God Calling You?" pamphlets needed to disappear if I was to marry Patty. There were nearly a dozen. This was mid-week; who was going to take all those pamphlets in one 24-hour period? I was crushed and immediately regretted my promise; but I was determined to fulfill my vow and trust completely in God.

The next day, I went to Mass and avoided looking at the pamphlets on the way in. When Mass ended, my heart was pounding. I loved Patty, but had told her nothing about my vow. I approached the pamphlet rack and searched. To my incredible relief, "Is God Calling You?" was not there. A quick scan revealed it was not in the rack at all. Curious as to what had replaced it, I picked up the new pamphlet from the upper left-hand corner and read the words "Building a Happy Marriage." There was no doubt that God was calling me to marry Patty.

Patty: I did not know of Tom's dilemma. I was too busy with the details of the wedding to notice that he was troubled. When he told me after we were married, I thought it was amusing. It's worth noting that my mom, whom I love dearly and who had paid for most of the wedding by the time of Tom's vow, got an uncomfortable (i.e., not quite as amused) look when we told her the story several years into our marriage.

The happiest day of my life was at the Easter Vigil Mass when I was baptized, confirmed and received Holy Communion. It was a glorious night! The second happiest day of my life happened five weeks later when I was united with Tom in the bond of Holy Matrimony. Those two events took place in the same church where I had attended my first Easter Mass, almost one year before. Everything had come full circle, from my dad's death to my new life in Christ.

I firmly believe that God takes something bad and makes something good come out of it. If Dad had not died, I probably would not have married Tom. I still miss my dad and wish that my children could have known him. Yet, I needed that difficult loss so my broken heart could be filled with a love that lasts eternally – God's love manifested to me through my husband, Tom.

Tom: The rash demand for a sign was the wrong way to resolve my quandary. Frankly, it is a little embarrassing that I punted on the most important decision of my life. But I was desperate. I had several reasons to consider a vocation to the priesthood. Marriage was the biggest decision of my life and the wedding was getting closer every day. I believe God bailed me out, in dramatic fashion, to jolt me from my habitual over-analysis. It worked. I haven't wasted a moment regretting my marriage to Patty. The entire experience illustrates how God works effectively through our weakness and sinfulness, when our need for a savior is most clear. As St. Paul said, "Where sin abounds, grace abounds more." (Romans 5:20.)

When I got down on my knees and prayed the Rosary for my future wife and children so many years ago, I could not have imagined how wonderful a marriage and family I would one day enjoy. This remains true, even as our only daughter is currently battling leukemia. Like any tragedy, a serious childhood illness can shake the foundations of married and family life. But for me, watching Patty care for her daughter the way she cared for her father only serves to remind me why I married her in the first place.

Patty: On May 23, 2011, we celebrated our 24th wedding anniversary. We have six beautiful children: Michael 22, James 21, Joseph 19, Mary 16, Christopher 14, and our adorable little five-year-old, Matthew. Tom's youthful solo prayer has become a symphony of mature prayers from our entire family; and one common intention is the vocation of each of our children and godchildren.

Like all marriages, we have our disagreements and disappointments, but we are happy. Year after year, we grow closer. Every aspect of our marriage, from our spiritual and social life together, to our physical relationship, is better than it was five years ago, ten years ago, and 24 years ago. God, indeed, answers prayers.

Tom is an attorney working for the U.S. Government. He has practiced a wide range of law, including criminal law, environmental law, government contract law, international law and torts. After graduating from law school, Patty worked as a clerk for several law firms and was offered an associate's position in two law firms, but declined because Tom's career took him away from the Washington, D.C. area. Patty is now devoted to being a mom and homeschools the youngest children. The Strunck Family lives in Charlottesville, Virginia with their six children ages 5 to 22.

The Strunck Family

Andrew Schmiedicke and Regina Doman

Married August 20, 1994

Our Fairy Tale Romance

Regina and Andrew 1994

Andrew: At 25 years of age I was already a lonely bachelor. After a number of failed relationships in high school, college, and after college; after a number of journeys, adventures, and failed business and employment ventures; I found myself back in Michigan, looking for a job, and feeling...well...like a failure. And a bachelor.

I prayed for my future spouse every day particularly seeking the help of the Holy Family and St. Raphael the Archangel. But at the time I had no means of supporting a wife and children. I couldn't even support myself. Fortunately, St. Raphael was also the patron saint of finances, so I thought he could help me with that too. Just after my 26th birthday, on the last day of a novena, I got a job working for a lawyer friend in West Virginia. Still, it didn't look like the job would either help me support a family or help me find a wife.

At the end of January 1993, I left West Virginia and drove up to Steubenville, Ohio. I spent the night with my sister's in-laws, the Nelson family. They said I could stay with them as long as I liked.

I stopped by to see my friend Mike. He was recently engaged to a girl named Alicia. He suggested I talk with Alicia's sister, Regina. She worked as an assistant editor at Lay Witness in New York City and might know of a job opening there. Sounded good to me. So Mike dialed the number.

Regina: At 24 years of age, I had never had a serious relationship. With my parents' encouragement, I hadn't dated at all in high school. "Focus on making friends and getting close to God," they had counseled. I was a good daughter, so I obeyed, and I was pretty glad that I did. Although I'd had a fair amount of crushes on different guys, I was saved a lot of heartache, and I had made a lot of friends. But even though I occasionally went to dances or out to dinner with guys, I tended to keep all men at arm's length. My senior year of college, I had dated casually, but the men I was drawn to always seemed to be discerning the priesthood or already in a serious relationship.

I was trying to convince myself that I had done the right thing in rejecting early dating, but sometimes it was tough. Like when I took a job far away from my large family and circle of friends and felt terribly lonely. Like when my younger sister Alicia got engaged to be married. I was trying hard to trust that God really did have someone for me, but I was always afraid that I'd end up in a no-man's land between marriage and the sisterhood.

As someone who thrived on having a goal, it was a depressing prospect.

I liked my job, working in an office in New Rochelle and traveling into New York City to go out to eat or to the theatre, but I spent most nights alone in my rented rooms. Eventually I moved my personal computer into my office and sometimes spent the night working away on a manuscript for a young adult novel. I would make a ramen-noodle dinner on the employee hot plate, lock myself in the office after the building alarms were turned on, and type away until I fell asleep on the floor.

One person I actually got closer to after I moved away was my sister's fiancé, Mike, a handsome and loquacious Irish-American who lived on nearby Long Island. When he was home from college, sometimes I would drive out to visit him and his family and we would hang out. But one day I was surprised to receive a phone call from him when I was at work.

"Hey, I have a friend who's looking for a job, and he's a good writer, and I know you work as an editor. Is it possible you might have a job opening for him?"

"Uh, I don't think we're hiring," I said, "but we could always take his resume..."

"Here, talk to him yourself," Mike said. "This is my friend Andy."

And then a deep, rich masculine voice, said, "Hello?"

I winced for the guy: it was clear he had been put on the spot. "Hi," I said. "So you're Andy? I knew your younger brother in college."

Andrew laughed – he had a nice laugh. "Yes, everyone knows him," he acknowledged. His younger brother had been a prominent pro-life activist at our college, spending time in jail for leading protests to save unborn babies. I had prayed for his brother, sent him a letter when he was in jail promising prayers. But I had no idea he had an older brother.

Andrew and I chatted for a few minutes, and he promised to send his resume, but both of us knew it was just a gesture. Mike probably wants to get his friend a job here in New York so he can have friends close by, I thought.

After I hung up the phone, I said to the secretary who shared the office with me, "That guy had a really nice voice."

Andrew: I sent my resume to Regina in New York, but nothing came of it, just as I guessed.

So I moved in with the Nelsons and got a handyman job with an old acquaintance. And I met with my spiritual director, Father Giles Dimock, O.P., about my vocation: priesthood or married life? He recommended I ask God for clarification about that on a retreat. So I scheduled a weekend retreat at the Holy Family Hermitage, a Camaldolese Monastery.

Father Giles counseled, "Try imagining yourself as a priest; then as a married man. Pay attention to what thoughts or feelings you experience during those imaginations." When I was alone in the small stone chapel, I approached the altar and imagined myself as a priest offering the Mass. I thought I would experience a rush of joy...But I didn't. I felt awkward and out of place.

Then I imagined myself at Mass with my future wife and children by my side. I was filled with happiness and felt a strong desire to be with that woman who would be my wife. So I felt certain that this was the direction God was leading me in.

Thinking hard, I genuflected, left the chapel and returned to my retreat cell, pondering. *How was I to support a wife and family?* I couldn't exactly do it by just being a handyman or a legal assistant. I had a desire to work in the church as a teacher of theology or a Director of

Religious Education, but I didn't have a degree in theology and I didn't have money to pay for – *Wait a minute! If the Nelsons really will let me stay with them free of charge as long as I need, I won't have to pay college room and board. And maybe I can get loans to cover the tuition. It just might work.* I left the retreat with renewed hope.

Returning to Steubenville, I asked the Nelsons if I could continue to live at their home while I pursued a Master's Degree in Theology. They generously said I was welcome to. And after I was awarded the Disciple of Christ scholarship, I knew I had a definite direction in my life.

Shortly after this I was reading a journal called *Caelum et Terra* and came across an article by the same girl I had spoken to in New York, Regina Doman. The article was titled, "The Church as One Big Rowdy Family," and I enjoyed it. I submitted an article of my own to the journal, but ended up getting in a rather heated disagreement with the editor about it. I told my friend Mike a little about the argument and he suggested I talk with Regina about it since she regularly contributed to the magazine.

Regina: In between writing my novel, I found time to write some freelance articles on the side for different publications that interested me. One was a journal called *Caelum et Terra* which championed farming, Catholicism, and the simple life. I became friends with the editor, and we corresponded frequently. Since he had protested the Vietnam War and my own dad was a decorated vet, I was pretty sure our relationship wasn't going anywhere, but he was fun to write to. In one of his letters he told me about this intellectual argument he was having with one of his contributors, Andrew Schmiedicke. So when Mike told me that Andy was frustrated with the editor of *Caelum et Terra*, I had a good idea of what he was talking about. That summer I was going up to a conference at Steubenville. Since Mike and Andy were working in the area that summer, I agreed to meet with them both at a restaurant on Sunday after the conference.

The Steubenville Youth Conference had been a source of

conversion for me when I was a teen, and even as a youth group leader, it was a lot of fun. But by Sunday, I was hot and exhausted, not to mention a little rumpled from sleeping on the ground and having lost my luggage. During one of the sessions, I saw Mike come into the tent followed by a guy wearing a white dress shirt and jeans of the palest faded blue. His longish dark hair was hanging over his eyes. I rolled my own eyes. Clearly, the guy didn't know how to dress. I was introduced to Andrew Schmiedicke and we shook hands, but given how loud the music was, we didn't have a chance for conversation. We agreed to meet at a local restaurant for brunch.

Andrew: When I spoke with Regina, she was dressed in a blue denim jumper with a white t-shirt, and her hair was a little messy. Regina was very easy to talk to, but I didn't feel the slightest hint of a romantic interest. I suspected she might be one of those girls who didn't care about her appearance very much.

But we had a great conversation about simple living, and the proper use of technology. In fact, we talked pretty much non-stop the entire time, while Mike and Alicia sat listening with smiles on their faces. It was clear Regina and I had a lot in common, especially being writers, but I really didn't feel attracted to her. I think it was mutual.

Regina: After the weekend in Steubenville, I could admit that I found Andrew Schmiedicke very intellectually interesting. I began to be curious about him, but I wouldn't say I was attracted to him. In the weeks after our meeting, my thoughts became consumed with the plans for my sister Alicia's wedding, which was taking place in January. This was our large family's first wedding, and Alicia and I had already spun out all sorts of plans to make it unique, romantic, and fun. Since I was always involved in party planning for our family, (and I was the maid of honor), I had a lot to do.

Alicia wanted to do things for Mike too, and that meant we had to involve the best man in the wedding who just happened to be... you guessed it, Andrew Schmiedicke.

This gave me an excuse to call Andrew fairly frequently. We would chat on the phone while I bounced ideas off of him, and explained the sort of things our brothers wanted to do for Mike for the wedding: we wanted the groomsmen to throw him a "bachelor bath" party which was the male version of a bridal shower: it involved the men of the wedding party praying and honoring the groom-to-be-after soaking him to the skin in a watergun attack. Andrew was keen to help out and take the lead, so plans were made.

So I was thinking about Andrew, but not romantically. I was glad he was happy to be a partner in the goings-on of our large, enthusiastic family. I was thinking of him that summer, when our family and a dozen other families made our typical joint vacation down to Cape Hatteras, North Carolina. Those ritual family vacations were almost a retreat, with daily prayer times together, skits, dinners, and beach games. Many of the girls I had gone on vacation with for the past ten years were dating and almost engaged. I was still (sigh) single.

My usual strategy was to hang out with the young married couples instead. I had always had friends of all ages, and I had no problem chatting with moms, holding babies, and playing with kids. One night when I was sitting on the couch in the beach house of one of my friends, I was watching a young dad play with his toddler son, and I thought to myself, *You know, that's what makes Andrew Schmiedicke different from these other guys I've dated. I bet he's the type of guy who would be a good dad.*

Those words had scarcely finished running through my head when one of the moms, Jane, looked at me keenly. "Regina, who are you thinking about right now?"

I blushed instantly. "Uh..." I faltered. "Just some guy I met this summer."

Looking intently at me, she said, "He's the one for you."

Andrew: Father Giles suggested I take a part-time job at the computer center on campus after I started classes. So

I started a job I was to keep for the next three years, where I gained valuable job experience that led to my first salaried position after graduate school, as well as to my current career. Even though I didn't realize it at the time, the financial part of my vocation was falling into place.

But as for the marriage part – nothing. No wife, no fiancée, no girlfriend, no dates. My attempts to get to know some of the Catholic girls on campus went nowhere. What was particularly frustrating was that I was attending a Catholic university where there were so many vibrant and wonderful girls. Couldn't one of them be the one I was looking for? And yet, it seemed that the elusive "she" was nowhere to be found.

Still, I was getting periodic phone calls from Regina regarding plans and events leading up to Mike and Alicia's wedding in January. I found that Regina, the oldest of ten, had a lot in common with me as the oldest of eleven children. We discovered that we both came from large and rather devout Catholic families. Our occasional conversations were pleasant, but didn't seem to go beyond that.

The week before Thanksgiving, I expressed my frustration to Father Giles. He told me to ask Jesus to bring the young woman into my life who was to be my wife. So I did. "Lord, if you want me to marry, bring the woman into my life!"

Regina: After vacation was over, I drifted back to New York City, still lonely, still working hard on the book I dreamed of someday publishing. As I wrote the romantic scenes between hero and heroine, I longed for some special connection of my own. But the future seemed very dark. I remember standing in the bathroom of my rented apartment one night and looking out at the night sky. "Lord, I'm just sick and tired of waiting," I whispered. "If you have someone for me, can't he come soon?"

I wondered if something might just work out between Andrew Schmiedicke and me. After all, we seemed to have a lot in common. But I felt uncomfortable calling him so often: I had been taught never to chase guys. I wished someone would chase me, for once. Someone I liked.

After ruminating over the problem for a while, I called Mike. "Hey," I said, "why don't you invite Andrew Schmiedicke to come to my parents for Thanksgiving with you?"

Mike appeared to be horrified. "Regina!" he exclaimed. "I could never do that! I would be a guest in your parents' home. I couldn't just invite a friend of my own along."

"But you could," I said, thinking of all the foreign exchange students and other assorted persons we had towed home with us during our college years. "My parents wouldn't mind. They always have lots of people over." My parents regularly had 20 or 30 people for Thanksgiving: with ten kids of their own and lots of relatives, they always said one or two more never made much of a difference.

"No," he said, "I wouldn't feel comfortable asking that."

"But Mike," I argued. "Andrew's going to be the best man. Doesn't he have to come to our house before the wedding, just to get the lay of the land, maybe find out where the church is?"

Mike sighed deeply. "Regina," he said. "the best man just shows up. He doesn't have to do anything except hand me the ring at the ceremony. There's no reason for me to ask him to come. And I don't know what Andy's plans are."

"Well, think about it," I said, a bit forlornly.

Much to my surprise, the next time I talked to Andrew on the phone, he said, "Hey! I've been invited to your parents' house for Thanksgiving!"

"You have?" I asked incredulously.

"Yeah!" Andrew said. "Mike was pretty intent on having me there. He said that since I'm the best man, there's all sorts of things I need to know. Like where the church is and stuff like that."

"Oh!" I said.

We were so clueless. Like I said, this was our first wedding, and we really didn't have any idea about what a best man had to do. And oddly enough in retrospect, neither of us picked up on what Mike was really up to.

Andrew: I was glad for the invitation to the Domans', but my melancholy mood was heightened during the six-hour drive. I had too much time to think, and it didn't help that Mike and Alicia were in the front of the car holding hands, and Alicia's brother, Martin, and his girlfriend Charlene were sitting in the back with me. Martin and Charlene snuggled and talked next to me while I stared out the window at the drab late fall scenery passing by. I felt like a fifth wheel.

On arriving at the Domans' house that night, I was warmed and impressed by the outpouring of mutual love and affection – so much so that I began wondering how I could become part of this family.

Later on, I was walking down the hallway where the Domans had dozens of framed family photos. One frame caught my eye: a large photograph of a lovely dark-haired young lady. The picture was hanging near photos of Alicia, Martin, and David – the older Doman children. I gazed at the picture of the young woman I didn't recognize and thought, "She is really lovely. I wonder who she is."

Was she perhaps an older sister I hadn't met or heard about yet? But no, I knew Regina was the oldest sister, and there weren't any sisters between her and Alicia. Was she perhaps a Doman cousin? But why would the Domans put a picture of a cousin with pictures of their eldest children? And not include their oldest daughter, Regina? That seemed odd. No, it couldn't be a cousin. I knew there were ten Doman children so I counted off the ones I had met. Finally, I looked at the picture and whispered,

"Regina?"

She looked so different in the picture, like a princess: her dark hair was smooth and stylish, and she wore a dark blue dress and pearls. When I had met her in Steubenville, she had seemed more like a plain peasant girl. Was she a princess in disguise?

Finally, I pointed to the picture and casually asked Mike, "Is that Regina?"

"Yeah," he said.

"Oh," I said. "Uh – why doesn't she wear her hair like that anymore?"

"I don't know."

Regina: I had gotten used to the drive from New York City to Pennsylvania: I would pray a rosary to start out the three-hour trip, then listen to tapes or sing songs. Driving through the darkness, I was glad to be getting home again.

Plus I was returning in triumph: I had finished the first draft of my novel! My brother Johnny was only fifteen but he was a budding writer himself, so I hoped he would read my printed-out story and give me feedback. Writers just yearn to be read.

And Andrew Schmiedicke was going to be there. I didn't quite know what I thought of him. I had to admit I was surprised I didn't have a crush on him. Well, crush or not, I was looking forward to seeing him. I'm pretty sure I prayed about him on the way home.

Andrew: That evening Regina arrived from her job in New York. After supper, Regina and her brother, John, who, I found out, was also a writer, were intently discussing something at the dining room table over a large pile of papers.

I asked them what they were talking about, and Regina

said it was a book she was working on, based on the Grimm's fairy tale called "Snow White and Rose Red."

"Oh, yeah," I said, recognizing the story.

"Not 'Snow White and the Seven Dwarfs,'" she said with a sigh. "It's a different one."

"I know," I said. "'Snow White and Rose Red.' It's one of my favorite fairy tales."

"Really?" Regina asked, surprised. She had taken note that not only did I know the story, but that I had listed it among my favorites and she therefore deduced that I was a person who, like herself, took fairy tales seriously. "Well, would you like to read my manuscript?"

"Sure," I said.

I started to read the story. It was engaging, but there were parts of it that were just too...flowery. Plus there were typos. I had grown up helping grade papers for my dad's English classes – he was a high school teacher – so I can't just let typos go. Not wanting to offend Regina, I asked for a pencil and corrected one small typo.

She was enthusiastic. "Oh, that's great! Please, go ahead, mark anything you think that needs to be changed. I won't be upset."

"Are you sure?"

"Sure."

"Okay then." I said, and slashed a line through several overlong paragraphs. "All this description has to go. It's too wordy. It stops me from enjoying the story, which really begins here..." I marked another place on the manuscript. "And this and this are redundant. We already know this information so don't restate it."

I looked at Regina, a little concerned that she might be

insulted. But she was impressed.

"Wow," she said. "Most people just say, 'oh, it's great. Better than I could do!' But this is really helpful! Please keep reading! And keep it up!"

We continued working on her manuscript until after one in the morning, both of us engrossed in the story. By the end of it I was sensing...something – I wasn't sure what – between us.

Regina: It was certainly the most interesting Thanksgiving Day I had ever had in my life. There was the usual hectic rush of cleaning and cooking and getting our massive holiday meal ready. But my holiday tasks were made a little easier because of the man who began following me around and helping me out with whatever I needed. When I cleaned the kitchen, he washed dishes. When I set the table, he folded napkins.

My siblings and relatives were mystified by him. "Is there something between you two?" they whispered to me whenever he left the room.

I could only shrug: I hadn't a clue.

One nagging wedding detail had been bothering me: I knew that for the bridal party dance, Alicia and Mike wanted to do swing dancing. My brothers, the other groomsmen, all knew how, but no one knew if Andrew knew how to swing dance. I doubted it. "Hey Mike," I said in passing to my future-brother-in-law. "Can you make sure Andrew gets dance lessons this weekend? My brothers can teach him."

"No problem," he said.

Andrew: After dinner, I was sitting on the living room sofa, looking at books with Regina and John, sipping wine and nibbling on bits of homemade pumpkin and apple pies. Martin had put on some jazz music by Harry Connick, Jr. and he and David were swing dancing with their respective girlfriends. Mike had told me that the bridal party would be swing dancing, but I was nervous: I didn't know how to dance.

When I confessed this, Martin and David offered to teach me.

So with Regina as my partner, David and Martin taught me some basic swing dance steps to Harry Connick, Jr.'s "It Had To Be You." I was thoroughly delighted. One might say "euphoric."

At the end of our last practice dance for the night, Regina and I, probably feeling a little giddy, gave each other a side hug. And smiling down at her, I suddenly knew.

I'm falling in love with her. That's what's going on! I'm falling in love with her! I'm sure a big goofy grin broke out on my face at these thoughts.

As I was going downstairs I continued thinking, *I'm in love with her. That's what's going on. I'm in love with her.*

Regina: As I was going upstairs to the girls' attic bedroom that night, I had to admit Andrew was cute. And helpful. And literary. But the truth was, he couldn't dance.

Andrew: The next morning the euphoria from the night before was gone. I was in just a regular, everyday emotional state. And yet, the calm, confident, deep sense of peace and knowing were still there. I knew I was in love with Regina, I knew I wanted to marry her, and I knew I was going to marry her. Even if she declined at first, I knew I'd convince her eventually. It was part of God's plan.

I knew the next thing to do was to tell Regina where I stood with her and what my intentions were. But the question was: Where, when, and how? I was only going to be at the Domans' for the weekend.

That presented another dilemma. Could I really tell Regina that I was in love with her and was planning on marrying her? We had known each other such a short time! Wouldn't she think that I was shallow and impulsive, acting on feelings caused by being thrown together for a few days? And, yet, I knew it wasn't just a fleeting feeling. I knew I was in love with her. I knew I was going to marry her. I knew that I knew. I had made the decision and I was totally at peace.

But how could I tell Regina that without scaring her away?

All right, I thought. *I can't tell her I'm planning on marrying her yet. If I did that, she'd probably just scream and run away. So it's too soon for that.*

How about I tell her I'm in love with her? Hmmm. Better, but it sounds a little too certain and shallow. She might get the impression I make a habit of falling in love with girls after spending a weekend together.

What can I say that is true and accurate that won't scare her away or give the wrong impression? Holy Spirit, I need a little help here!

And then it came to me. I would just tell her that I was *falling* in love with her. Yes, that was it. I had fallen in love with her, but I was also continuing to fall in love with her. It was true and it would give the impression of something that had recently begun and was continuing (both true) without giving the impression that it was all wrapped up and I was planning on marrying her next week – which I would have. But there was no need to scare her off with talk like that even if it was true.

Now I just needed the perfect time and place to tell her.

Regina: It probably wouldn't surprise you to learn that I'm considered the clueless one in my family. Yet after another day with Andrew, I could tell something was going on. Hoping that he had something to tell me, I kept thinking of excuses for us to go off together alone on some errand. But he never said anything. When I invited him to go on a walk with me on Friday night down to the creek near our house, and he was quiet the whole time, I began to think he was just painfully shy.

And I thought I knew what I would have to do next. I'd have to be straightforward with him. I'd have to ask him directly. My heart sank. I'd had to do this before, when I sensed a guy liked me. I always hated doing it. It made me feel too pushy. But if that was what Andrew needed, I resigned myself to doing it.

Andrew: Saturday night, I asked Regina, "What time does your family go to Sunday Mass?"

"They usually go to the 10 a.m. Mass," she said.

"Oh good," I sighed. "Then I can sleep in a bit."

"Well, actually," Regina said a little awkwardly, "I was wondering if you would be interested in going to an earlier Mass with me, and then going out to breakfast afterward."

I was pleasantly surprised. "Sure." *An opportunity to speak to her privately*, I thought.

During Mass the next morning I kept praying things like, *Jesus, please help me love Regina the way you love your bride, the Church. Please help me love her the way you want me to love her. Please help me tell her the way you want me to. Please let me know when to tell her.* Over and over again I prayed this silently in my heart. When I received Jesus in Holy Communion I prayed even more fervently as I walked back to the pew with Regina. I was not nervous or anxious. Rather, even as I prayed with my whole being, I was at peace and confident – my spirit embracing and embraced by the Holy Spirit.

As Mass ended, Regina whispered to me, "I usually pray a decade of the rosary for my family after Mass. An 'Our Father' for my parents and one 'Hail Mary' for me and each of my brothers and sisters. Would you pray that with me? We can pray for your family too."

"Sure," I said. So we knelt down and put our heads near each other, whispering the prayers so we didn't disturb the other people around us.

During the prayers, I kept listening to the Holy Spirit, and knew it was time.

As we finished the prayers for our families, I leaned toward Regina and whispered, "I suppose it's rather obvious, but I'm falling in love with you."

Regina: My mind went completely blank. I was so surprised I sat back down. I couldn't think of anything to say. I just sat there, whispering "I can't believe it. I can't believe it. Wow." I was vaguely aware of Andrew sitting next to me in the pew, grinning, apparently delighted at having caught me off guard.

My plan had been pre-empted, but I couldn't have been happier.

Silently, Andrew put his open right hand, palm up, into my lap. I stared at it, then quietly put my hand in his. It was a man's hand, tough, firm, and strong. Exactly what I had been looking for, longing for.

Andrew: We left the Church hand-in-hand and walked through the drizzle to Regina's car. Just before reaching it we stopped, faced each other, and spontaneously embraced. Moments passed. Droplets of water fell from the soft gray sky sprinkling onto the deserted parking lot and trees, enveloping us in a mantle of mist. Still we stood.

Finally, Regina, with her head against my chest, said quietly, "Well, something must be happening, because we're just standing here in the rain."

Regina: Eventually, we did get to breakfast, at a vintage 50's diner in my hometown. There I pressed Andrew for his further intentions. Sure, we had just had a romantic interlude, but where was it going? What did it mean?

I'd had this sort of thing happen before: a guy tells me he thinks he's in love with me, but then a week later decides that the Holy Spirit is actually leading him in a different direction. Determined not to get caught in another emotional wilderness, I asked, "Where does our relationship go from here?"

Andrew at this point did actually know exactly where our relationship was headed, but afraid of scaring me away with talk of marriage so soon, he said a little vaguely, "Well, I'm just going to continue to listen to the Holy Spirit and follow His lead."

This was EXACTLY what I did not want to hear. So, like any assistant editor, I gave him a deadline.

"Well, you have to take the lead in this relationship. I'm not going to do it. So you have to let me know what you want. I'm coming to Steubenville next weekend for a surprise party for Alicia. You think about it this week and let me know if you want to date me or not."

Andrew seemed to be fine with that. "Okay," he said with a smile.

Andrew: That week I had a confirmation that my relationship with Regina was of God and that it was meant to lead to marriage. A Franciscan friar who was teaching my sacraments class was talking about discerning one's vocation. He said there were three signs to look for.

1. A constant desire for a particular state in life.
2. A knowing that you know.
3. A deep sense of peace.

All of which I had experienced.

So when Regina and I met again in Steubenville the weekend after Thanksgiving she asked, "So did you make a decision about what you want in our relationship?"

"Yes. I would like to date you. I would like it to be an

exclusive dating relationship. We don't date anyone else," I said firmly.

"Good. Because that's what I want too," Regina replied. We were on the same page.

This was also the point at which our telephone bills dramatically increased. The post office got a lot more of our business too. Regina would write me letters the length of small dissertations. I, on the other hand, was already writing papers and essays for school. Although I wrote her at length when I could, my letters to her were shorter. Sometimes I even had to resort to postcards signing off with "In haste, your knight in fading blue denim." No shining armor here. All I had was an old jean jacket. I thought of her as my "princess in disguise," a line from her manuscript, since she dressed so plainly, yet the picture in her parents' house had clued me into the fact that she was really a princess.

By the time of Mike and Alicia's wedding on January 8, Regina was thoroughly and obviously in love with me. And I – to Regina's delight – could dance. At the wedding reception, she and I had a wonderful time swing dancing to "It Had to Be You."

After we got engaged as the result of a misunderstanding (for full details, please see my book, Our Fairy Tale Romance), we set the wedding date for August 20, 1994 and bought rings at a Michigan antique shop.

During a silent and solitary retreat the weekend before our wedding, I composed our marriage consecration prayer that we recited at our wedding ceremony. We renew that consecration once every month on the date of our wedding anniversary.

Regina: Of course I planned our wedding – down to the very last detail. I wore a dress I had designed my junior year of high school, based on a simple white day dress Queen Marie Antoinette had worn, with a lace-ruffled neckline, puffed sleeves, and a light blue satin sash. I braided pink satin roses on ribbons in my hair. My bridesmaids, my four sisters and four of Andrew's sisters, each wore a different pastel color of the rainbow. Andrew and I had fun pairing up our various younger brothers and sisters together for the wedding party. We had chips and hot dogs for the wedding reception held in a college cafeteria so that we could invite everyone we wanted to – and all their kids. It was a real family wedding, and we were proud of that for years, the kids who attended said it was the funnest wedding they had ever been to.

But on the wedding weekend, I stopped answering the phone and on the wedding day, I stopped answering questions. I didn't want to worry about the place-cards or the flowers or the videographer or any of the numerous things that might or could go wrong. I was determined that on my wedding day, all I was going to do was wake up, pray, get dressed, and get married. The rest of it would take care of itself.

To this day, I'm glad I made that choice. Yes, there were glitches and messes on the wedding day, but they didn't matter. The sacrament was what mattered.

Andrew: I was so thankful when the wedding day finally dawned. I felt like something my whole being had been yearning for my entire life was finally coming to fulfillment after much wandering, prayer, and searching.

Our wedding was a celebration of life – we had about two dozen people in the wedding party and about 400 guests...plus their children. The Mass was a harmonious blend of traditional and charismatic songs and music with guitars, flutes, piano, harps, and violins. Mr. and Mrs. Nelson read the first reading from the Book of Tobit telling the story of how St. Raphael the archangel brought Tobiah and Sarah together in marriage after many sufferings and difficulties. My spiritual director, Father Giles Dimock, gave the homily and the nuptial blessing.

At the reception, Mike and Alicia came up to us and confessed that they had conspired together to set us up to meet in the first place, thinking that we might hit it off. They were delighted that their matchmaking succeeded so spectacularly.

After the reception, some time towards early evening, Regina and I changed out of our wedding clothes and disguised ourselves once again as a plain peasant girl and a poor knight in fading blue denim. I then picked Regina up into my arms and carried her through a storm of confetti, cheering people, and balloons as we made our way to my black metal steed (my pick-up truck). We got in, and waving goodbye, drove off into the setting sun...happily ever after.

*Andrew earned an M.A. in Theology from Franciscan University of Steubenville. After a fairy tale romance, he and Regina Doman married in 1994. In 1996 Andrew and his brother Mike founded a web development company, Veraprise, with a partner. (www.Veraprise.com). In 1999 Andrew began producing a radio drama version of Regina's first book called **The Shadow of the Bear** which won the 2009 "Best Audio Drama Show" award from the Sonic Society (www.ChestertonProductions.com). "He's the secret of my success," says Regina. Andrew has been working with Regina as a freelance agent/editor to develop Catholic fiction for Sophia Institute Press, in order to foster a greater sense of Catholic identity (www. CatholicTeenNovels.com) among youth and young adults.*

Andrew and Regina have had eight children so far: seven of whom are still living with them near Front Royal, Virginia, where they make their home at Shirefeld Farm raising lambs, llamas, chickens, and a pig or two.

Regina began writing stories by the time she was five. Eventually, she obtained a B.A. in Communications and moved to New York City where she worked as an assistant editor, and wrote columns and articles for various publications. After a fairy tale romance, Regina married her husband, Andrew, in 1994. With his enthusiastic encouragement and support, she began publishing her fairy tale novels for teens in 1997 (www.FairyTaleNovels.com). Her picture book for children, Angel in the Waters (www.AngelintheWaters.com), has sold over 100,000 copies. She is the creator and managing editor of the John Paul 2 High series (www.JohnPaul2High.com) for teens published by Sophia Institute Press for whom she also reviews and edits fiction manuscripts (www.CatholicTeenNovels.com).   In addition to writing and editing, Regina homeschools her children, does arts and crafts, helps her husband raise sheep, llamas, and chickens, and also speaks at conferences, schools, and workshops. To the question, "How do you manage to get it all done?" Regina responds, "What makes you think I get it all done?" (www.ReginaDoman.com)

Regina and Andrew

Acknowledgments

The editors are grateful to the 12 couples who so generously agreed to share their courtship/dating stories with us. This has been a true labor of love for us.

We would also like to thank our excellent copy-editors, Cheryl Thompson and Jeanette MacDonald.

A special thank you to Latitia Martin and Timmy Hrkach for helping with the cover. Thank you also to our capable team of proofreaders: Jeanette MacDonald, Ginger Regan, Cheryl Thompson, Ingrid Waclawik, Sue Atkinson, Tom Strunck and Louise Waclawik.

We also ask readers to check out the following websites of our contributors:

Regina Doman's websites
www.FairyTaleNovels.com
www.AngelintheWaters.com
www.ReginaDoman.com
www.JohnPaul2High.com
www.CatholicTeenNovels.com

Andrew Schmiedicke's websites
www.ChestertonProductions.com
www.Veraprise.com

Damon and Melanie Owens' websites
www.joyfilledmarriagenj.com
www.njnfp.org

James and Ellen Hrkach's website
www.fullquiverpublishing.com

Ellen Gable Hrkach's websites
www.ellengable.com
www.emilyshope.com
www.innameonly.ca

Sarah Reinhard's website
www.snoringscholar.com

David and Rosalie Douthwright
www.madonnahouse.org

To order more copies of this book, please go to

www.comemybeloved.com

**or to the Full Quiver website
www.fullquiverpublishing.com**

or buy directly from Amazon.com

Appendix

Natural Family Planning
by Damon Owens

Natural family planning, or NFP, is an umbrella term to describe natural methods of achieving, postponing or avoiding pregnancy that monitor naturally occurring signs of fertility and infertility in a woman. Many credible methods exist to train couples to practice NFP successfully in marriage, and all share high effectiveness and a marriage-building challenge to love "as God loves."

NFP is Fertility Intelligence (FI), that is, the ability to "read from within" a woman's fertility, and Responsible Parenting (RP), the right moral use of this knowledge. We cannot fully understand one without the other: the biological signs witness to a deeper meaning and vocation of the body-person, and our theology of personhood is made visible in the reading of the language of the body. NFP for the married couple must include Responsible Parenthood, which, building credibility from FI, addresses the most difficult question of "how" we are to use justly the knowledge of our fertility in the vicissitudes of marriage to fulfill our call to marital holiness.

NFP is a tool to keep our shared gift of fertility "front and center." It elevates the horizon of our sexual desire from an experience in time to include the possibility and the mystery of an act of love that could live forever as a new soul.

For more information on Natural Family Planning, check out the following websites:

www.ccli.org
www.serena.ca
www.woomb.com
www.joyfilledmarriagenj.com   www.njnfp.org
www.creightonmodel.com

Do you have any interesting, inspiring or humorous courtship/dating story?

Did you and your spouse meet in an unusual way?
Do you find yourself sharing the story of how the two of you met?
Is your story particularly inspiring?

Full Quiver Publishing is working on a second book of Catholic courtship stories.

If you would like your story to be included in our next book, or if you want more information, please contact us at:
info@fullquiverpublishing.com

Write "courtship stories" in the subject line.

About the Editors

Ellen Gable Hrkach is wife and mother, freelance writer and award-winning author of three novels. She can be found online at www.ellengable.com and at various other websites. She is the Vice President of the Catholic Writers' Guild. She and her family currently live in Pakenham, Ontario Canada.

Kathy Cassanto is a wife and homeschooling mother who runs a home baking business. She and her family live in Braeside, Ontario Canada.

The editors gladly welcome feedback about this book. Please contact them at info@fullquiverpublishing.com

Copies of this book can be purchased on Amazon.com and at www.comemybeloved.com

Full Quiver Publishing
PO Box 244
Pakenham ON K0A2X0
Canada